Five Ancestor Fist Kung-Fu

FIVE ANCESTOR FIST KUNG-FU

The Way of Ngo Cho Kun

Alexander L. Co

Charles E. Tuttle Company
Rutland, Vermont & Tokyo, Japan

Published by Charles E. Tuttle Publishing,
an imprint of Periplus Editions (HK) Ltd.

LCC Card No. 97-60011
ISBN 0-8048-3153-X

First Tuttle edition, 1997
First printing, 1998

Printed in Singapore

Distributed by:

USA **Charles E. Tuttle Company, Inc.**
Airport Industrial Park
RR1 Box 231-5
North Clarendon, VT 05759
Tel: (802) 773-8930
Fax: (802) 773-6993

Japan **Tuttle Shokai, Inc.**
1-21-13 Seki
Tama-ku, Kawasaki-shi
Kanagawa-ken 214, Japan
Tel: (81) (44) 833-0225
Fax: (81) (44) 822-0413

Southeast Asia
Berkeley Books Pte Ltd.
5 Little Road #08-01
Singapore 536983
Tel: (65) 280 3320
Fax: (65) 280 6290

Tokyo Editorial Office:
2-6, Suido 1-chome,
Bunkyo-ku, Tokyo 112, Japan

Boston Editorial Office:
153 Milk Street, 5th Floor
Boston, MA 02109, USA

Singapore Editorial Office:
5 Little Road #08-01
Singapore 536983

DISCLAIMER

Please note that the author and publisher of this book are NOT RESPONSIBLE
in any manner whatsoever for any injury that may result from practicing the techniques and/or following the instructions given within. Since the physical activities
described herein may be too strenuous in nature for some readers to engage in
safely, it is essential that a physician be consulted prior to training.

Visit Tuttle Web on the Internet at:
http://www2.gol.com/users/tuttle

To the memory of my late master
Sifu Tan Ka Hong
for his loyal teachings, supervision, and technical editing
of this translation of his notes

Table of Contents

Introduction

Unlike other Chinese fighting arts, the ngo cho kun system of kung-fu is relatively unknown in the United States—though it is well known and highly popular in Southeast Asia. The relative anonymity of ngo cho kun in the Western world should not be construed as an indication of the style's lack of credibility. Ngo cho kun appears hard, brisk, and brutal in character—quite atypical of the soft, light, graceful, but lethal movements normally associated with kung-fu. Yet, ngo cho kun is no less a Chinese fighting art. Compared with other kung-fu styles, the system is non-classical and devoid of "flowery" technique. It is the combat application of the techniques that lies at the heart of this fighting art.

Ngo cho kun, or "fists of the five ancestors," is a Shaolin martial art from Fukien province, China. It consists of techniques from five different styles: peho (Fukien white crane), kao kun (monkey boxing), Tai Cho (grand ancestor boxing), lohan (Buddha boxing), and tat chun (Tamo's method). Created by Sijo Chua Giok Beng in Chuan Chiu, Fukien province, ngo cho kun was brought to the Philippines by Sigung Tan Kiong Beng, a direct disciple of the founder. For over fifty years, the art was propagated by Sifu Tan Ka Hong, the son of Sigung Tan Kiong Beng, and the art's second-generation grandmaster. Sifu Tan founded the Beng Kiam Athletic Club, the oldest Chinese martial arts school in the Philippines.

Ngo cho kun makes extensive use of the hands for attack and defense, a short stance, and pressing steps to overwhelm an opponent. Leg techniques, considered secondary tactics, are found in the form of kicks, sweeps, and scissors take-down maneuvers. Iron-body training is also an important feature of the system; it conditions the practitioner's body to prevent pain and serious injury.

What is striking about this Fukien style, is the startling similarity in principles and techniques to Okinawan karate. Indeed ngo cho kun is accepted by some as the source from which several systems of modern

9

karate have evolved. Goju-ryu, Uechi-ryu, and Isshin-ryu karate all share a common form, *sanchin*, which is the Okinawan adaptation of the ngo cho kun form, *sam chien*. In addition, the Shotokan karate concept of *ikken hisatsu* (one-punch kill) was also probably derived from ngo cho kun. Unlike kung-fu styles that advocate defeating an opponent with a flurry of blows, ngo cho kun stresses the reliance on a few powerful techniques. A practitioner of ngo cho kun will typically move close to an opponent in an effort to smother his defenses and instantly conclude the encounter. It is a highly realistic and practical fighting art.

As a martial arts enthusiast and publisher of the Philippines' *Martial Arts Magazine*, I have had the opportunity to meet a wide variety of martial arts masters. As a collector of martial arts books, with thousands of titles in English, Chinese, and Japanese, I have come to understand their importance in preserving the arts. Although several books have been written on the style of ngo cho kun in Chinese, there is no single authoritative book on this discipline. It is hoped that this current work fills that void.

This is the first authoritative text on the art of ngo cho kun. As the art spread from its origins in China to Southeast Asia, there naturally developed a number of collateral styles with variations in the execution of techniques. In total, the art consists of forty-four forms, twelve weapons, strength and conditioning training, pre-arranged fighting drills, and free-sparring practices. The contents of this book are derived from the lineage of Master Tan Ka Hong whose father, Tan Kiong Beng, was a direct disciple of the founder, Chua Giok Beng. Due to space limitations, however, it is impossible to include the entire system of ngo cho kun in a single volume. I have, therefore, chosen to present here the most basic and important form, *sam chien*. It is considered the mother of all ngo cho kun forms, and from it is derived the nucleus of all ngo cho kun techniques. This form is so important, that Master Tan always stated: *"Lien kun sam chien ki, sam chien, lien kaw si,"* which roughly translates to "Begin your training by practicing *sam chien,* and don't stop practicing *sam chien* until your very end." In addition, *in tin tat,* a more advanced ngo cho kun form, is also included to show the diversity of techniques in this art.

This book was written with the permission, support, and cooperation of my late master, Sifu Tan Ka Hong. His generous permission to translate and copy from the "master text" (which is written in Chinese and was handed down to him from his father), is a great contribution toward preserving and perpetuating the art of ngo cho kun. When Sifu Tan passed away in 1990, he left behind his legacy in the form of a series of manuscripts on the art of ngo cho kun. Included in these essays is the *Tiong Hua Yu Sut Tai Tsuan* (Complete Chinese Jujutsu), which is considered by many to be the Bible of ngo cho kun. I hope in the near future to translate this book into English and make it available as a reference for all kung-fu and karate enthusiasts.

The research committee at the Beng Kiam Athletic Association helped me to compile the reference material for this book. In 1983, I translated the "master text" into English. In an effort to reach a wider audience I published the book in both English and Chinese in the Philippines. Then, in 1996, at the urging of Mark Wiley, I rewrote and expanded my original book and submitted it for publication to Tuttle Publishing.

A concerted effort was made to present to the readers the most accurate English translation of this obscure text. As some Chinese characters have no direct translation into English, I chose the corresponding words which most closely render their original meaning. In addition, the original Chinese characters appear next to the words in the glossary for a more accurate translation. I believe this English translation to be at once clear, concise, and effective in conveying the essence of ngo cho kun.

I would like to note that this book is the result of group coordination and cooperation. For their research assistance and editorial help with the earlier version of this work, I extend my deepest gratitude to my sihings: Alfonso Ang Hua Kun, Willy Keh, Leonardo Co, Vicente Go, Alexander Ong, Henry Gan, and Bonifacio Lim. In addition, I am grateful to Christopher Ricketts for taking the time to pose opposite me in many of the photographs; to Mark V. Wiley for editing and restructuring my original work into this current form; and to the Charles E. Tuttle Company for their willingness to publish it.

If this book has generated your interest in the art of ngo cho kun, then my work has not been in vain. Join me now in a lifelong journey to explore this dynamic Chinese fighting art.

— Alexander L. Co

Binondo, Manila

PART ONE

General History

1

The History of Ngo Cho Kun

INTRODUCTION

Ngo cho kun is one of the most popular styles of kung-fu hailing from Fukien province, China. (The style is known as ngo cho kun in the Amoy dialect; in Mandarin, it is known as wu chu chuan). Long the pride of Fukien province, ngo cho kun has since spread to other Asian countries including Malaysia, Singapore, Vietnam, Burma, Indonesia, the Philippines, Japan, and Hong Kong.

During the Chinese revolution, many of the top kung-fu masters fled their homeland, emigrating to various countries in Southeast Asia. In the Philippines, the renowned ngo cho kun masters have made their mark. The late master Lo Yan Chiu (nicknamed "Tiger" Chiu) propagated his version of the art through his Kong Han Athletic Club, which was situated in Binondo, Manila's Chinatown area. Until his death, Master Tan Ka Hong was the highest authority on ngo cho kun in Southeast Asia, and headed the Beng Kiam Athletic Club, also situated in Binondo.

SIJO CHUA GIOK BENG

The roots of ngo cho kun can be traced to Sijo Chua Kiam, also known as Giok Beng and I-Ho. Chua Giok Beng was born in 1853, in Fukien province, amidst the turmoil of the declining years of the Ching dynasty (1644–1911). He lived in the village of Pan Be, a few miles from the city of Chuan Chiu. Raised in a wealthy family, Beng's parents were engaged in the sauce manufacturing business. They owned a sauce garden, which is where Chinese food is processed by immersing it in a salty sauce. Despite the business's increasing prosperity over the years, Beng's heart was with the practice of kung-fu. To him, material and monetary gain was secondary to the practice of martial arts. Beng's intense desire to learn kung-fu led him to be accepted as a pupil of venerated master Ho Yang, a native of Honan province. Beng's lessons were conducted in the sauce

師祖蔡玉鳴先生遺像

拳打八洛
嬌如神龍戲水

腳踏四門捷如猛虎翻山

天師證讃

武科領峻
高來北助
功

神龍矢蟄
公門桃李

人雛西去
薪傳妙技
師首犬堯

一字玉鳴
國術尤精
集其大成
久著威名
隨地句餘
道猶帝行
播及海瀛
永留英靈

Sijo Chua Giok Beng

garden, thus enabling him to utilize his time efficiently. When Ho Yang died of old age, it was Chua Giok Beng who escorted Yang's remains to his hometown province of Honan. On his journey back, Beng took the hard route; he wandered throughout China for ten solid years, continuously searching for new techniques and ideas, practicing and combining them until he created a composite style of kung-fu which he considered the perfect fighting art. This style is ngo cho kun, or "fists of the five ancestors."

In creating his new style, Beng combined the five distinctive techniques from the five styles peho (Fukien white crane), kao kun (monkey boxing), Tai Cho (grand ancestor boxing), lohan (internal Buddhist boxing), and tat chun (Tamo's iron-body training). The peho style consists of a variety of hand techniques. Ngo cho kun's hand movements, arm movements, and finger strikes often resemble the wings of a crane, as they are patterned after peho techniques. The kao kun style offers ngo cho kun many evasive tactics such as jumping, dodging, and dropping into low, squatting stances. The palm strikes of kao kun are likewise incorporated into ngo cho kun. The Tai Cho style was named after Sung Tai Cho, first emperor of the northern Sung dynasty (A.D. 960). He reportedly practiced a system that featured numerous jumping, sweeping, and scissors-kick attacks. These same leg techniques are a part of advanced ngo cho kun training. The lohan style is an internal kung-fu system, relying on short steps that serve as the basis for ngo cho kun's footwork. It is also recognized as the original form of Shaolin boxing. Finally, the tat chun style forms the basis of ngo cho kun's iron-body training. The Indian monk Tamo introduced the *Muscle Changing Classics* (*Yak Kun Kieng*, in Fukien; *Yi Chin Ching*, in Mandarin) and the marrow washing exercises (*swe che kieng*, in Fukien; *shi sui ching*, in Mandarin) to the monks at the Shaolin Temple. These exercises were adapted to condition the ngo cho kun practitioner's body.

After spending his entire fortune on his odyssey through China, Beng returned home. Not surprisingly, the family business, with nobody to attend to it, had closed. Dispassionate over the loss of material wealth, Beng concentrated his body and mind on the study of kung-fu. He opened a kung-fu school called Lin Gi Tong (Hall of Humanity). On its door hung a sign which read: "Gentlemen, let us study the way of *sam chien*, and warrior, please observe my *ngo ki lat* (five parts power)." In addition to teaching kung-fu, Beng also made use of his medical knowledge by offering his services to the community. As was the custom, many masters from different schools came to challenge and test Beng's art. The Sijo went undefeated, becoming so well-known in his region that he soon earned the moniker Mua Lo Hiong (Popular all the Way).

Chua Giok Beng was a man of peculiar character—unworldly, and disinterested in the glitter of riches and wealth. To Chua Giok Beng, kung-fu was the heart and soul of being. In his forties, Beng had passed the government test for *bu siu chai* (a post in the military) with flying colors. This examination tested one's expertise in shooting arrows while astride a running horse. Instead of accepting a position in the government, Beng chose to continue his pursuit of kung-fu. This was during the decline of the Ching dynasty. Since corruption was rampant in the government, Beng felt he could not compromise his integrity. Instead, he rose to greater heights in the field of kung-fu and became well known for his *pat wat* (eight methods deadly technique).

Sijo Chua Giok Beng was also an expert in both the iron palm *(ti sha chiong)* and light body *(kin gung)* methods. It is said that he could effortlessly leap to the roof of a two-story house in a single bound. As a result of this amazing acrobatic feat, Beng became known as Pan Be Ho, or the "Crane of Pan Be Village." His reputation spread throughout Fukien, and many masters of other styles came to study under him, consequently incorporating ngo cho kun into their respective styles. Anyone who had a specific ability in kung-fu was welcomed by Beng and invited to stay in his house. Beng's house in Pan Be had no doors, only windows—anyone possessing the ability to jump from the ground to the window of his house, was welcomed as an honored guest.

In his last years Beng was a nomad, wandering from one place to the next. Shunning materialism, he dressed in ragged clothes. If Beng

Sigung Tan Kiong Beng

received new clothes or money, he offered them to the destitute, making him a philanthropist of sorts.

In Chuan Chiu, Chua Giok Beng's first students became known as the "Ten Tigers of Ngo Cho Kun." They included Kiu Lu of Chuan Chiu (also known as Kao Sai), Yu Chiok Sam of Kuan Kio, Wei Bun Pa (also known as Wan Tian Pa), Lok Te Kim Kao, Bicho Seller, Phoenix Hand Ho Hai Sai, Tan Tao Sai, Hong Kiao Sai of Ching Yong, Kua Chai Hun Sai, and Tan Kiong Beng Sai (also known as Golden Wings Tai Peng). Each became famous in their own right, some for their specialty techniques, others for their extraordinary feats. They were held in high esteem and revered. Thus, people from the nearby regions came to study under them.

SIGUNG TAN KIONG BENG

Sigung Tan Kiong Beng is the first-generation master of ngo cho kun under Sijo Chua Giok Beng. Nicknamed Tai Peng, Tan Kiong Beng was born in Chuan Chiu to a wealthy, business-oriented family. Gifted with a strong physique, Beng could easily lift a sculptured stone lion weighing 500 pounds a considerable distance from the ground.

During those times, it was customary for rich families to employ the services of kung-fu experts to teach in their mansions. Normally, rich families hired the most noted kung-fu practitioner of the time. At that time,

Sijo Chua Giok Beng was the most noted kung-fu master, and was thus hired by Tan Kiong Beng's family as their private tutor. Tan Kiong Beng's family was highly privileged and honored to have Giok Beng as their private instructor. Since Tan Kiong Beng was a man of noted moral character, he was accepted as the direct "in-door" disciple of Chua Giok Beng. Though he learned much of what Chua Giok Beng knew, Tan Kiong Beng's thirst for knowledge could not be quenched. Tan followed his master in the latter's sojourn throughout China and absorbed the complete system of ngo cho kun. After more than ten years of continuous, devoted training, Tan also became a master. Under the discipleship of Master Beng, Tan Kiong Beng became skilled in the iron palm technique *(ti sha chiong)*, and widely acknowledged for his expertise in the "roc-spreading-its-wings" technique *(tai peng)*—a combination which made him unbeatable. As a result of his proficiency in the arts, Tan was given due recognition as one of the "Ten Tigers of Ngo Cho Kun."

Aside from his expertise in the martial arts, Tan was also adept in traditional Chinese medicine. When Tan opened his own clinic in Chuan Chiu, Master Giok Beng blessed him with the authority to name the clinic Lin Tek Tong (Hall of Humanity), after the old master's own club. Like Sijo Beng, Sigung Tan's first love was kung-fu. He practiced often and devoted the remainder of his time to his clinic. Though many were after his knowledge, Tan held dear the quality of his students rather than their quantity, and only taught his closest friends.

Sometime in 1918, Sigung Tan Kiong Beng visited the Philippines and offered his services as a doctor to his fellow Chinese friends and acquaintances. His knowledge in the martial arts did not pass unnoticed among local kung-fu enthusiasts. Prompted by numerous requests from eager friends, Tan taught his art to a select few. To this day his skills in ngo cho kun and traditional Chinese medicine are well remembered.

SIFU TAN KA HONG

Until his death in 1990, Sifu Tan Ka Hong, the son of Tan Kiong Beng, was the leading exponent of ngo cho kun, not only in the Philippines but around the world. Sifu Tan Ka Hong grew up in a family embedded with kung-fu influence and traditions. In addition to having a father who was an expert in ngo cho kun, his mother was a practitioner of the peho style, and the daughter of Fukien white crane master, Ong Kue Seng.

Sifu Tan Ka Hong learned the rudiments of kung-fu at the age of seven through the patient teaching of his mother. He divided his study time between school and kung-fu. When he reached eleven years of age, Hong's father began teaching him ngo cho kun, but under a strict regimen. After more than ten years of arduous practice, Hong achieved complete mastery of the art, including its complementary healing tradition.

Sifu Tan eventually met Master Kim Chian, a disciple of Shaolin kung-

Sifu Tan Ka Hong

fu, who later taught Tan the empty-hand techniques of the Shaolin style, along with various weapons including the sword, staff, spear, and knife. This comprehensive instruction greatly expanded Hong's horizons to include both the northern and southern Shaolin kung-fu styles—a perfect blend of arts complementing each other.

Although few, the recorded exploits of ngo cho kun are impressive. In 1934, Chang Tze Chiang, the president of the Nanking Central Kung-Fu Institute, went with a group of kung-fu experts to Manila to promote Chinese martial arts through exhibitions and dialogues with local kung-fu clubs. Ngo cho kun Master Sijukcho Chang Hun Chiong, together with some old students of Sigung Tan Kiong Beng, participated as performers in the kung-fu exhibition. For the first time, the local audience was treated to the astounding power of the five arts of ngo cho kun.

Sijukcho Chan Hun Chiong was a scholar and a kung-fu expert. Being an "in-door" disciple of Sijo Chua Giok Beng, Chiong was able to absorb the styles and techniques of the old master. He relocated to Manila to assume the principal seat at the Tiong Se Academy. Although Sijukcho Chang Hun Chiong came to Manila to assume a career in education as principal of the Tiong Se Academy (one of the oldest Chinese schools in Manila), word spread that he was also an expert in ngo cho kun. As a result of the warm reception and interest in ngo cho kun shown by martial artists, he was deeply inspired to open a club. Chang Hun Chiong wrote Sigung Tan Kiong Beng, presenting him with the bright prospect of opening a club in the Philippines, while at the same time inviting the old sifu to visit and spearhead the art in that country. Already in his later years, Sigung Tan Kiong Beng felt that he did not have to personally go to the Philippines. Acknowledging his complete trust in Sifu Tan Ka Hong, his closest disciple, Sigung Tan sent his son to the Philippines to fulfill the task required of him. On the eve of his departure, Sigung Tan made Ka Hong swear before the altar to observe the following oath:

I will advance the art of ngo cho kun
I will respect and follow the rules and tenets of the style
I will always treat people with respect and humility of character
I will exercise morality and pulchritude at all times

In 1935, Sifu Tan Ka Hong relocated to Manila and was warmly received. The organization of a kung-fu club was immediately discussed. Sijukcho Chang Han Chiong suggested that since Sijo was known as Chua Giok Beng, they should name the club Beng Kiam in honor and the memory of its founder, thus perpetuating the master's name for posterity.

After World War II Manila was in ruins, and the formerly active Beng Kiam Club was in need of resurrection. Sifu Tan Ka Hong gathered the people devoted to ngo cho kun and reestablished the Beng Kiam Athletic Club. Beng Kiam was eventually able to build its own house, establishing solid roots in the Philippines.

Forty-eight years later, Beng Kiam is still a name to be reckoned with in the Philippines. Moreover, it is revered among ngo cho kun clubs throughout the world. Beng Kiam has turned out hundreds of students with the able support of its directors, under the supervision of Master Tan Ka Hong. Its students have spread to other parts of Asia, some making it to the United States and other countries.

The Beng Kiam house still stands today. Though already old, Beng Kiam's interior bespeaks of ancient Chinese kung-fu traditions, with an

Front row: Tan Ka Hong *(seated center)*, Alfonso Ang Hua Kun *(kneeling left)*, the author *(kneeling right)*. Standing from left to right: Tan King Tong, Benito Tan, Bonifacio Lim, Willy Keh, Andy Ong, Leonardo Co, Henry Gan, Vicente Go

Sifu Tan Ka Hong *(seated)*, Alfonso
Ang Hua Kun *(right)*, Benito Tan *(left)*

altar at its center and various weapons at its sides. Through the years,
Beng Kiam contributed to the local Chinese community through giving
kung-fu exhibitions and demonstrations. Similarly, Master Tan Ka Hong
offered his knowledge of traditional Chinese medicine to the local Chinese community in Binondo, Manila.

In his capacity as a master, Sifu Tan Ka Hong was close to his students
and treated them with kindness and fatherly concern. This reflects the
Chinese tradition of a close, yet strict, master-disciple relationship. When
Tan Ka Hong passed away in 1990, he did not officially designate anyone as heir to the system, although at one point he asked me and Leonardo Co if we were interested in assuming the responsibility of carrying on
the tradition. After more than fifty years of teaching, there were many
practitioners senior to us, but during his last years there was no one clos-
er. While I continue to help run the Beng Kiam Athletic Association, my
senior kung-fu brother, Alfonzo Ang Hua Kun, was granted permission
from Sifu Tan in 1990 to open his own club, the Tsing Hua Ngo Cho
Kun Kung-Fu Center. The name Tsing Hua was chosen by Tan Ka
Hong—a customary gesture that the master approved the opening of
one's own kung-fu club. The term *tsing* means "to excel," Hua is taken
from Alfonzo's name. When combined, the term *tsing hua* means
"essence," (e.g., the essence of ngo cho kun kung-fu). Although other
senior members have since opened their own clubs, they never received
the blessing of Tan Ka Hong. Thus, they are not recognized by Beng
Kiam, the senior club. Hua Kun stands as the only disciple of Tan Ka
Hong permitted to open a collateral ngo cho kun club. As a result, it is
Hua Kun who is carrying on the tradition of ngo cho kun as the fourth-
generation master, following in the footsteps of the Beng Kiam Athletic
Association and the late Master Tan Ka Hong.

2

Reminiscences of Tan Ka Hong

The following two essays were written by the late Sifu Tan Ka Hong. The first was written under the pseudonym Hong Ho, and appeared in the *Beng Kiam Souvenir Annual* of 1956, published in celebration of Beng Kiam's twenty-first anniversary. The second was written in 1971 for the souvenir program of Beng Kiam's goodwill mission to the People's Republic of China.

CHUA GIOK BENG AND HIS NGO CHO KUN

Pugilism (kung-fu) is one of the best sports of our country. Ngo cho kun stands out as one of the most popular among the different styles of kung-fu from southern Fukien. Ngo cho kun is made up of Tai Cho kun, lohan kun, tat chun kun, peho kun, and kao kun. These five styles each have their own respective advantages: Tai Cho kun specializes in *chang chuan* (long fist boxing); lohan kun specializes in whipping strikes; kao kun specializes in agile legwork; peho kun specializes in clever techniques. By integrating the essence of these styles, Chua Giok Beng crafted ngo cho kun which has developed into a distinctive style in its own right. Although the form looks like Tai Cho, it also resembles kao kun and peho. That is why many northern kung-fu masters are confused as to what style ngo cho kun belongs. Many of the popular *kun-to* (forms) such as the *sam chien* (three wars), *se mun* (four gates direction), and *song sui* (double banner fist), fall under ngo cho kun, thus establishing this art as a legitimate style in southern Fukien.

The founder of ngo cho kun is said to be the famous Chua Giok Beng, who came from Chuan Chiu during the late Ching dynasty. He was a native from the Pan Be village of Chin Kang prefecture. Prior to becoming a martial arts scholar (official) Beng was already famous as a kung-fu master throughout the five prefectures of Chuan Chiu. People called him

23

Pan Be Ho (Crane of Pan Be). After he became an official they all called him Beng Lo (Venerable Beng).

It is said that as a youth, Chua Giok Beng was gallant and quite fond of kung-fu. He made many friends with masters of both the northern and southern styles. As a result of his training, in a few years he had spent the fortune left to him by his father. After ten years of traveling around the country, coupled with his intelligence, Beng was able to learn many different styles from several well-known masters. Along the way, as he heard of many famous teachers, Beng would approach them for instruction. After just a few years, Beng became an expert in various northern and southern kung-fu styles. After that, he combined his knowledge and founded the famous ngo cho kun.

Although already quite famous in Chuan Chiu, it wasn't until his midyears that Beng returned to his hometown—this time as the founder of a new style. Many kung-fu experts went to challenge and test his skills. Not one of them could best Beng. That is why his fame echoed through southern Fukien, and why Beng was recognized as an eminent authority among the southern Fukien kung-fu circles. Famous masters in Chuan Chiu, such as Wei Lin Pa (Wan Tian Pa) and Lim Kiu Lu (Kao Sai) of the Tai Cho style, became Beng's student after their defeat. Lim Kiu Lu, a strong and muscular master of the *chang chuan* (long fist) style of Tai Cho, was already a famous teacher and only one year junior to Chua Giok Beng. When Lim tried to test his skills with Chua Giok Beng, he was sent back several feet by the power of Beng's punch. Admiring his skills, Lim Kiu Lu quickly became Sijo Beng's student.

When Wei Lin Pa heard of Lim Kui Lu's defeat, he could not believe it and went to challenge Chua Giok Beng himself. Being an expert in kicking techniques, Wei Lin Pa attempted to sweep Chua Giok Beng, but was instead grabbed by Beng and thrown through the walls of the house. During those times, the walls were constructed of reeds and saw dust cemented by mud, thus being somewhat brittle. As a result of this encounter Pa also became Beng's student.

In the southern Fukien kung-fu circles, Chua Giok Beng was nicknamed Mua Lo Hiong (Popular all the Way). This was because he had so many students, and everyone was trying to become his student. Chua Giok Beng was welcomed everywhere with open arms. While in his middle-age years, because of the number of students paying homage to him, Beng had few troubles with his life. In his older years, Beng always wore a faded blue coat, and no matter what his students gave him in terms of new clothing, he never seemed to take it off. His students wondered what he did with all his new clothes. Later on, they discovered Chua Giok Beng's peculiar trait; that is, he always wore the new clothes beneath the old ones. Since he never carried money with him, when he encountered a person in need, he would instead take off the new clothes and give them away.

Chua Giok Beng never had any intention of taking the exam to become a county martial arts official. As a result, he never paid much attention to archery and horse riding. Later on, however, in Chuan Chiu, there were many martial arts scholars who admired his extraordinary skills and they persuaded Beng to learn the art of archery and horsemanship, in order to undergo the examination. At that time Chua Giok Beng was already forty years old. He passed the test and became a *bu siu chai* (martial arts county official).

At that time, there was no master in Fukien province who could defeat Chua Giok Beng in hand-to-hand combat. As a result, many of the established masters came to study under him and were thus influenced by ngo cho kun. Such influence made ngo cho kun one of the most popular styles in China. In Chuan Chiu, and other nearby places, many adopted his *sam chien* form to the beginner's curriculum. Although the *sam chien* seems simple, with only three steps forward and three steps backward, these steps are the essence of ngo cho kun kung-fu.

THIRTY-SIX YEARS OF BENG KIAM

I remember that it was in 1935 when I travelled to the south of the Philippines to organize the Beng Kiam Club. It happened one early, spring morning thirty-six years ago. The flowers were blooming in the spring sunlight of our garden. I was practicing my kung-fu on that early morning when my father sent someone to call me to meet him in our living room. He then told me: "Some of my old students from the Philippines have repeatedly sent telegrams, asking me to go there again to teach kung-fu. But I am already old, and have passed my prime. Besides, I hope to spend my remaining days enjoying my home instead of traveling to foreign lands. But my students are persistent and I must propagate the art of ngo cho kun. So, I think it is better that you go in my place."

Upon hearing my father's request, I felt at once confused and excited because I knew that I was still young and in my kung-fu prime. But, the thought of leaving my father and going south to be someone else's teacher frightened me. Although I was afraid that I might not be qualified, I could not disobey my father's order. So, I packed my bags, which consisted of one broadsword and one flower-spear, and in March bought a ticket and sailed to the Philippines.

Upon reaching the port of Manila, I recognized only three people. During my welcoming party that evening, through Sijuk Chang Hun Chiong and Sihing So Bun Ching, I was introduced to Lim Tian Suy, Uy Sun Ki, and other *sihing* (kung-fu brothers). At once, we organized a committee to plan the formation of an association and discussed an appropriate name and place for it. As a result of being a student of Sijo Chua Giok Beng, Chang Hun Chiong was the kung-fu brother of my father. He was not only an educated scholar, but an expert in kung-fu. In 1919, Chang

The 1937 officers of the Beng Kiam Athletic Club with Master Tan Ka Hong (second from left), Sijukcho Chang Hun Chiong (center), and Lim Tian Suy (second from right).

became the principal of the Philippine Tiong Se Academy, and later assumed the post of secretary of the Overseas Chinese Education Bureau. Chang Hun Chiong suggested that since our style belongs to the famous Sijo Chua Giok Beng, we should name the association Philippine Beng Kiam Jujutsu Association.* After deciding on the name, we set out to find a location to house the association. Lim Tian Suy offered his place, a cigarette factory on Asuncion Street, as a temporary site. Lim Tian Suy was elected as the first chairman, with Chang Hun Chiong as the honorary chairman. Later, we borrowed the old Philippine-Chinese High School for our training grounds.

Tan Tiong Gong was unanimously elected as the second chairman of the association because of his dedication to it. Soon thereafter the Sino-Japanese War began. All of the members then felt that the name Beng Kiam Jujutsu Association sounded too Japanese, and suggested a change to the Beng Kiam Kok Sut Association. It later came to be known as the Beng Kiam Association under the leadership of Tan Tiong Gong, with the help of Tiu Heng Ying, Tiu Pieng Hong, Lim Tian Suy, Uy Sun Ki, and others. The association prospered rapidly as additional students joined. The association then moved the Su Kong Academy to Nueva Street, where it was more accessible to the students. As a result, student enrollment jumped to 400 members. We then began importing weapons

The author performing the *pin-ta* (peddler's staff) during a demonstration

A 1975 group exhibition (*author on the extreme right*, Hua Kun *in the center*)

from China, including the spear, broadsword, and halberd. In order to promote camaraderie within the kung-fu circle, we suggested the organization of a joint kung-fu exhibition with the different clubs. The exhibition was held at the Manila YMCA, marking the first-ever joint exhibition of this sort in the Philippines. The association became even more successful as a result. Later, it was moved again, this time to the old Su Kong Academy address on Soler Street. During the Sino-Japanese War, whenever there was a "grand meeting" of the overseas Chinese, our association was always invited to give kung-fu demonstrations. This is one contribution for which the association stands proud among the Chinese community.

In 1941, Japan invaded the Philippines. Officially, the association was closed and stopped its activities, with most of its members scattered into the mountains to escape the ravages of war. In actuality, however, many

The old Beng Kiam
Club, ca. 1956

of its members joined the guerrilla forces to fight the invading Japanese. This is another proud contribution of the association.

After the war, Beng Kiam was rebuilt. In February of 1945, Manila was liberated, but left in shambles. I initiated a campaign to rebuild the Beng Kiam Association by contacting the remaining members. Under the leadership of Tan Tiong Gong, the association was able to construct its own place on Nueva Street in October of 1946. After the war, aside from kung-fu, the association also promoted other sports such as badminton. The association's badminton team has won many championships throughout the years.

Ching Kiat Hwa, assuming the post of the eighteenth chairman of the association, devoted his time and money to further expanding its activities by organizing dragon- and lion-dance groups. He even led the group on a tour to the central Philippine island of Cebu to give exhibitions. The Beng Kiam Association then started to open relations beyond the Chinese community, promoting friendship with the Filipinos. The association also constructed a third-floor, in-door badminton court to promote this sport among the youth, developing future champions. To this day, Beng Kiam still holds the title of Philippines champion in badminton.

Ever since the establishment of the association I have always adhered to the principles of respect, humility of character, morality, and pulchritude, according to the association's creed of conduct.

Throughout the years, the members of the club have always treated one another with respect and brotherhood, living in harmony as an extended family. This I cherish deeply. Time passes so fast. In the a blink of an eye, thirty-six years have already elapsed. Through these nearly four decades, the survival and achievements of Beng Kiam are due to the collective contributions and sacrifices of all its members and officers. Taking advantage of the celebration of Independence Day in 1971, our association specially organized this Goodwill Mission, and published this souvenir annual. I am just an uneducated kung-fu practitioner, my educational attainment is not of a sufficient standard, but I rely on my devotion. I dared try to write a simple history to let the members have a better understanding of our association.

---

* During the early 1900s, just after the Boxer Rebellion, the Chinese people had a negative impression of kung-fu. At that time, kung-fu was called *kok sut,* an abbreviation of *tiong kok bu sut* (Chinese martial arts). People tended to identify kung-fu practitioners as *kun-hui* (fist bandits). This may also explain why Yu Chiok San titled his book *Tiong Hua Yu Sut Tai Tsuan* (Chinese Jujutsu Complete). This is also why Beng Kiam first adopted the term jujutsu, instead of *kok sut,* as its name. The Beng Kiam Jujutsu Association later changed its name, however, to the Beng Kiam Kok Sut Association. During those times, there was no direct translation for the term *kok sut,* so many kung-fu associations proceeded to simply identify their clubs as athletic associations. As a result, Beng Kiam is now officially know as the Beng Kiam Athletic Association.

3

Ngo Cho Kun and Okinawan Karate

INTRODUCTION

When tracing the roots of their respective styles, karate practitioners and historians alike have learned that karate was derived from fighting arts brought to the Ryukyu Islands, especially Okinawa, by Chinese merchants, pirates, and soldiers. In fact, one Okinawan style, Shorin-ryu, is actually the Japanese counterpart of Shaolin, believed to be the origin of kung-fu. The migration of martial arts from China to Okinawa was documented by legendary karate masters, who wrote of their expeditions to China to learn kung-fu. Because kung-fu is given credit for having spawned and/or influenced so many of the world's martial arts, karate historians are left wondering from which particular style of kung-fu karate originated. Although there are many styles of kung-fu, from the northern Shaolin styles of tang lang, kao kun, and ying jow pai, to the southern Shaolin styles of Hung-gar, choy li fut, wing chun, and pak mei, not one can boast of a consistent, broad-based similarity to karate. Similarities found are generally negligible.

However, two aspects of karate training do stand out as concrete clues in the search for the roots and ancestry of Okinawan karate. One is the highly regarded kata, *sanchin,* of which some masters claimed came from China in their search for higher learning; the other is the widely-used *sai,* commonly known as a karate weapon of self-defense.

FUKIEN'S SHAOLIN TEMPLE

Kung-fu researchers know that, aside from the famous Shaolin temple located in Honan, there were several other Shaolin temples throughout China. One of these was a temple in southern China located in Pu Tian, Fukien, which was believed to have been burned down by Ching soldiers. This led to the dispersal of the temple monks and gave rise to the legend of the Five Survivors, later worshipped by the Hung Men (a triad society) as the Ngo Cho (Five Ancestors). One of the survivors was the monk Chi-San, believed to be the teacher of Hung Shi Kwan. It is of interest to note that Hung Shi Kwan, a native of Fukien, escaped from the Manchus and traveled to Canton, there establishing the foundations of the famous Hung-gar (tiger-crane) style of kung-fu, named after his surname.

Although Fukien province boasts of great fighters like Hung Shi Kwan, it was not known as a good place to study kung-fu. One reason for this is that the people of Fukien were more inclined to scholarly pursuits than physical activities such as kung-fu. This is in contrast to the people of Canton, where martial arts were popularly practiced by all. Consequently, most kung-fu styles flourished in Canton, which later became known as a melting pot of most major kung-fu styles.

The existing styles of kung-fu popular in Fukien include peho (Fukien white crane), chuka (southern Shaolin styles), te bok sut (dog style), fu jow pai (tiger style), chua kun (snake style), and ngo cho kun (five ancestors fist). Although all of the styles are practiced in China today, the two of interest to us here are peho and ngo cho kun. These styles were later almost fused into one system because of their great similarities in theory and technique. Both styles eventually found their way to other countries, and do in fact hold the closest resemblance, in training and techniques, to Okinawan karate, particularly the Goju-ryu and Uechi-ryu systems.

NGO CHO KUN'S INFLUENCE ON KARATE

During the eighteenth-century, Chinese merchants traveled to Okinawa, bringing with them various aspects of Chinese culture, including the practice of kung-fu. The Okinawans were exposed to an advanced form of fighting far superior to their indigenous Okinawa-te. In fact, it was customary for serious practitioners of Okinawa-te to go to China in search of higher learning in the fighting arts. The exploits of these masters is best described in Richard Kim's book *The Weaponless Warrior*, and Shoshin Nagamine's book, *Tales of Okinawa's Great Masters*, in which are presented the history and masters of Okinawan karate.

In *The Weaponless Warrior*, Kim recounts the story of Kanryo Higashona, the teacher of Chojun Miyagi, the father of Goju-ryu karate. Kim talks about Higashona's journey to China, specifically his travels to Fukien. There he was taught the art of kung-fu by a Chinese master for more than ten years. The emphasis of the teaching was the famous kata, *sam chien* (now known in karate as *sanchin*). He also describes the incredible power of Kanryo Higashona, including his "unchokable" neck. Kanryo had his students tie a rope around his neck and allowed them to pull the rope to try to choke him. They were unsuccessful. Kanryo also challenged students to try and move him from his "immovable" stance, the *sanchin dachi*. These characteristics, the unchokable neck and immovable stance, *sanchin* kata and *sanchin dachi*, are the core of ngo cho kun.

Chojun Miyagi became a serious student of Higashona and followed in his footsteps. He too went to China to further his knowledge of the martial arts, leaving his family's fortune behind. Miyagi's stint in China has been subject to numerous speculations and conclusions. Karate historians claim that he studied the internal style of pa kua, and through this learned the importance of the soft style. Miyagi concluded that a complete martial art should contain a combination of hard and soft techniques, thus giving rise to his particular style, Goju-ryu, or the "hard-soft" style.

However, history books and interviews gathered from old masters during those times reveal that pa kua was practiced only in the northern part of China. Also, kung-fu was highly regionalized and was taught with the utmost secrecy and restriction, making it almost impossible for a foreigner like Miyagi to learn it in any other part of China. Consequently, it seems likely that Miyagi studied kung-fu not in the northern part of China, but instead in the central or southern regions. The reason many people felt Miyagi learned pa kua was due to the similarity of his style's knife-hand block and pa kua's single change palm. One of the most controversial debates among karate historians pertains to the validity of the story that Miyagi actually studied pa kua in the central or southern areas. This is of course very hard, if not virtually impossible, to prove. The most valid theory seems to be that Miyagi, in his quest for further learning, traveled to China and later settled in the central or southern region. There he did learn kung-fu, not the pa kua style but rather ngo cho kun, whose movements, principles, and techniques have come to be duplicated in karate, thereby making it the father of many Okinawan karate systems.

While there are perhaps an indefinite number ways in which kung-fu has influenced Okinawan karate, the following are but ten examples of karate techniques that were borrowed from ngo cho kun (depicted here by the author and Christopher Ricketts). There are several ways of categorizing these techniques, but for the sake of simplicity, they are grouped into three categories: high-level techniques, mid-level techniques, combination high-and-low level techniques.

Examples of high-level techniques include ngo cho kun's double open-hand outside block *(sang tioh chiu)* and karate's double outside forearm block *(morote chudan uke)* (Fig. 1); ngo cho kun's whip strike *(pian)* and karate's backfist strike *(uraken uchi jodan)* (Fig. 2); ngo cho kun's center-arm on-guard position *(tzi ngo tiong ki)* and karate's on-guard position *(kamae)* (Fig. 3); ngo cho kun's enticing hand *(chiao yung chiu)* and karate's knife hand block *(shuto-uke)* (Fig. 4); ngo cho kun's double grabbing block *(sang kim)* and karate's double hooking block *(morote kake-uke jodan)* (Fig. 5).

Examples of mid-level techniques include ngo cho kun's finger strike *(cha)* and karate's spearhand strike *(nukite)* (Fig. 6); ngo cho kun's dou-

Fig. 1

Fig. 2

Fig. 3

Fig. 4

ble open-line block *(sang kwi sua)* and karate's double wrist strike *(morote yoko koken ate)* (Fig. 7).

Examples of high-and-low level techniques include ngo cho kun's holding the shield technique *(po pai chiu)* and karate's tiger-mouth *(tora-guchi)* (Fig. 8); ngo cho kun's rocking strike to the groin *(yaw)* and karate's groin strike *(migi shuto gedan uchi-komi, hidari sho migi kata ue*

Fig. 5

Fig. 6

Fig. 7

Fig. 8

nagashi uke) (Fig. 9); ngo cho kun's high and low block *(lohan chiu)* and karate's simultaneous high and low block (from *kate sochin, muso gamae)* (Fig. 10).

A COMPARISON OF KATA

The kata taught by Miyagi are the *sanchin* and *tensho*. The *sanchin* of Goju-ryu is notably similar in principles and movements to the *sam chien*

Fig. 9   Fig. 10

of ngo cho kun. The movements and principles of the kata *tensho* are also strikingly similar to ngo cho kun, and it seems these similarities are by no means coincidental.

Uechi-ryu, another major Okinawan karate style, also bears striking resemblance to ngo cho kun. In the early 1900s, Uechi-ryu karate founder, Kanei Uechi, Sr., traveled to Fukien province to further his skills in the martial arts. While there, Uechi supposedly learned a kenpo style known as pangai-noon. However, current research indicates that there never was a style known as pangai-noon. Conversely, pangai-noon refers to the Fukien Amoy dialect term, pan-ngi-nang, which means "half-hard, half-soft." Presumably, through the passage of time, the style eventually came to be known as pangai-noon in Okinawa, as teachers taught their students the importance of being both hard and soft in the execution of their martial movements.

Another explanation is that Uechi's teachers may have camouflaged the name of their style so Uechi could not disclose the true identity of this secret system. It is believed that what he learned was actually ngo cho kun. Like Goju-ryu, the principles and movements of Uechi-ryu are exceedingly similar to those of ngo cho kun. Again, the similarities are by no means coincidental.

Yet another interesting comparison is the high regard Okinawan karate and ngo cho kun place on the practice and perfection of kata. Karate practitioners believe the *sanchin* kata is the heart of their system; likewise for the practitioners of ngo cho kun. What appear to be simple, basic movements are actually abbreviations of inner, hidden movements. To understand this, we must analyze the kata as practiced in both Fukien province and Okinawa.

In both ngo cho kun and Okinawan karate, the kata assumes a perfect circle, the beginning is the end, the end is the beginning. The student begins and ends his training with *sanchin/sam chien.* By studying the form, the student is exposed to its movements, which to him are simple and basic. The movements may appear to be just preludes, or preliminary steps to higher forms of learning or technique, but in reality, *sanchin/sam chien* is the core of ngo cho kun, Uechi-ryu, and Goju-ryu. Every movement in these systems derive their roots from this form. In order for a student to become proficient in either Okinawan karate or ngo cho kun he must know this form. Once he passes this fundamental form, he progresses to a higher form, where he is taught the different movements and techniques hidden in the seemingly basic *sanchin/sam chien* form. In reality, the *sanchin/sam chien* form holds the key to all the advanced techniques. The student begins to see how these simple movements provide the clues to discover greater techniques and thereby aspires to know more and seek a deeper understanding of the movements. The importance of this form may be likened to the roots of a tree: without its roots, a tree is lifeless, dead. The roots are the sustaining power of the tree; this form is the life and sustaining power of ngo cho kun, Goju-ryu, and Uechi-ryu.

With regard to weaponry, the *sai* has been popularly regarded as an Okinawan karate weapon. However, the principles and techniques of the *sai* are of Chinese origin. The *sai* is actually a primary weapon of ngo cho kun, where it is known as the *sang te pi.* The basic reason it was not associated with kung-fu was that southern styles like ngo cho kun were kept secret, which was typical of ancient Chinese tradition. The styles of kung-fu which were able to find their way to the Western world and receive some recognition were those styles which were propagated in Canton. These styles did not use the *sai.* It was, therefore, an uncommon weapon until Miyagi developed and subsequently spread his system. Hence, through the passage of time, it came to be known as a karate weapon.

It is hoped that with the presentation of the art of ngo cho kun that follows, one will gain a deeper insight into the relationship between this art and Okinawan karate.

PART TWO

The Foundation of an Art

4

Fundamentals of Practice

Behind the simplicity of the ngo cho kun lies great practicality. Behind the simple techniques lay vast secrets of fighting. Ngo cho kun techniques exploit the full potential of its practitioner's strength, thereby making it a true pugilistic art. The efficacy of the techniques, however, is dependent on the practitioner's ability to develop and maintain proper form, stances, and footwork in coordination with the five parts power.

PROPER FORM

When teaching ngo cho kun, Sijo Chua Giok Beng placed emphasis on three components: breath *(chi)*, form *(sze)*, and strength *(li)*. He stressed that if these components are properly cultivated, one's kung-fu skills will develop naturally. In addition, by properly cultivating and combining spirit *(ching)*, breath *(chi)*, and soul *(shen)*, power will also develop naturally. However, Beng's primary emphasis was on form *(sze)*. Without proper form the practitioner is believed to be like a puppet, pulled and controlled by a string. Lacking proper form, the practitioner, while moving forward and backward, will lack the grace and posture of the style. In ngo cho kun, proper form is not only necessary but essential.

Proper form is assumed by combining various elements. The clenched fist must be half yin and half yang (i.e., held diagonally). The feet should hold the practitioner firmly to the ground. Just as the foundation of a tree comes from its roots, the source of strength emanates from the soles of the feet. The ears should be sharp to detect even the slightest blowing of the wind. The eyes should be aware of the four directions of the human gate: left and right, back and front. As a ngo cho kun maxim states: "Motionless, the practitioner serenely manifests the gentleness of a lady; actively he personifies the agility of a rabbit."

Fig.1

Fig.2

Fig. 3

Fig.4

STANCES

The dynamic strength and ferocity of ngo cho kun techniques require the stability of strong stances. The foundation of this art is grounded in four basic stances: the t-stance *(chien be)*, level horse stance *(si pieng be)*, hanging-leg stance *(tiao-be)*, and bow-and-arrow stance *(kieng tzi be)*.

The hallmark of ngo cho kun is its primary stance, the *chien be*, which accommodates the system's footwork. Drilled and practiced to perfection, this stance protects the groin, strengthens the legs, and allows for mobility. Breathing exercises in the *chien be* stance allow a higher retraction of the testicles, affording the practitioner a safety margin when encountering groin kicking attacks.

The *chien be* stance could be regarded as one of the greatest inventions of Fukien Shaolin kung-fu. This seemingly simple stance is the essence of ngo cho kun, the secret to developing strength through *chi,* and the premiere tool in the development of one's physique.

To assume the *chien be* stance (Fig. 1), place one leg in front of the other, with forty percent of the weight on the front leg and sixty percent on the back leg. Then, tuck in the buttocks, allowing the spinal column to form a straight line from the tip of the head, thus forming an unobstructed pathway for the passage of *chi.* The knees should be drawn inward, and the testicles drawn upward.

The level horse stance *(si pieng be)* (Fig. 2) is assumed by standing with the feet parallel and the knees drawn inward. Weight is equally distributed between the legs.

The corner stance *(kak be)* (Fig. 3) is similar to the *chien be* stance, except for the direction in which the practitioner is facing. When assuming the corner stance the practitioner faces sideways.

The bow-and-arrow stance *(kieng tzi be)* (Fig. 4) is similar to the front stance used in karate. Weight distribution is seventy percent on the front leg and thirty percent on the back leg. The front foot is turned slightly inward.

FOOTWORK

Ngo cho kun makes use of short steps when moving from one point to another. While the steps may be short and swift, they actually carry such a grounded weight that they are able to crush a head. The following are the different steps of ngo cho kun.

The direct forward step *(tit chin po)* is initiated from the *chien be* stance by first stepping forward with the front leg (Fig. 5), then dragging the

Fig. 5   Fig. 6

Fig. 7   Fig. 8

Fig.9   Fig.10   Fig.11

rear leg behind (Fig. 6). The direct backward step *(tit-teh)* is performed in reverse by first stepping back with the rear leg, then dragging back the forward leg.

The forward step, simply called "step-on" *(ta-po)*, is used to move into the *chien be* stance from the level horse stance. This is done by either moving one foot forward or backward (Figs. 7, 8).

The double forward step *(tiap chin po)* is initiated from the *chien be* stance by first moving the left foot forward (Fig. 9), followed by the right foot (Figs. 10, 11). The double backward step *(sang tit-teh)* is performed in reverse by moving the left foot backward, followed by the right foot.

Fig.12   Fig.13   Fig.14

Fig.15

The overlapping step *(tap be po)* is initiated by stepping the left foot over the right foot (Figs. 12, 13), and then stepping sideways with the right foot (Fig. 14). This is similar to the double step, but is performed in a crisscross fashion. The evading overlapping step is performed by moving to either side rather than to the front.

The crouched kneeling step *(kut be po)* can be assumed from any stance, and is performed by repositioning your feet and dropping to one knee (Fig. 15).

Fig.16

The hanging leg step *(kia ka po)* is performed by retracting the lead foot to avoid an oncoming attack. This is achieved by placing ninety percent of your weight onto the back leg, with ten percent of your weight on the tip toe of the front foot (Fig. 16). This stance is generally used to retreat by jumping back or to pursue by jumping forward.

Other methods of movement include stepping to either side, jumping directly forward and backward, or a spiral turning jump to either evade an attack or to bridge the gap between you and your opponent.

FIVE PARTS POWER

Ngo cho kun's five parts power *(ngo ki lat)* refers to the head, both hands, and both feet. When simultaneously using all of the five parts, connected by the trunk, the dynamic of the entire body is put into each strike.

The head should be held upright, the chin sunk low, the mouth slightly open while retracting the lips to tense the facial and neck muscles, thus simulating the form of a crying rooster. To complete the fierce look, the eyes are held wide open, like the eyes of a big fish, the tongue is curled to touch the upper palate, the muscles at the sides of the lips are tensely pulled back, and the nostrils are expanded. Each inhalation and exhalation of breath should produce the quiet sound of a tiger's growl. With a single look, the practitioner, in such a state of facial contortion, looks like a beast ready to devour its prey. The frontal three parts of the body include the chest (expanded), the hips (tucked in for proper alignment of the spine and easy passage of *chi*), and the testicles (tucked in, with concentration focused on the *tan tien*). The practitioner is then ready to engage his opponent in the center-arm, on-guard position *(chi-ngo tiong ki)*, the classical fighting stance of ngo cho kun.

The power source of the hands is divided into three parts: the shoulders, elbows, and wrist. The first power source is derived from the shoulders, which should droop, sinking the chest inward. You should feel the weight going down to the buttocks. The second and third power source are derived from the elbows and wrists respectively, the key words being *tun* (swallow) and *toh* (spit out). The elbows are held at the sides of the torso (i.e., swallow), while the forearm, wrist, and hand are held in such a way as to mimic the slope of a dust pan (i.e., spit out). When the hands are thrust forward or backward, with the shoulders drooped and the forearms tucked to the sides, the hands will vibrate as a result of muscle tension. Chinese kung-fu masters liken this force to a "dragon playing in the water." Exhale when you thrust your hands forward, inhale when you retract your hands to your sides. The continued inhalation and exhalation uses *chi* to produce power and strength. The third power source is derived from the upper torso, by twisting and shaking the shoulders and trembling the stomach. Before thrusting the hands out, pull them in to gain momentum so that when you thrust, there will be a vibrating sound from your strength. This vibrating sound is intrinsic energy *(nei-ching)*. Internally, you are hard as steel, but externally you are soft as cotton—thus maintaining an equilibrium of hard and soft, yin and yang. The body, though hard and flexible, is like a wheel when turning. The stomach is as hard as a steel wall.

When assuming a proper stance, the legs should be firmly anchored to the ground to achieve and maintain stability, while allowing fast and agile footwork. The stance's power source is comprised of three segments: the upper legs or thighs, the lower legs or shins, and the feet. When focusing training on these three parts, you should will your mind to circulate the *chi* by way of inhalation and exhalation, with it passing from one leg to another as if in a continuous cycle. In the three segments of the legs, the thighs are tucked in, the ankles are exposed outwardly, and the toes are curled up to tense the calf muscles, with the soles of the feet glued to the ground. With the proper form, every step will automatically be firm, like roots in the ground. This forms a solid stance, thus making the ngo cho kun practitioner as immovable as an iron bar. Diligent practice will enable one to move with ease and coordination while maintaining stability and power.

5

Basic Techniques

INTRODUCTION

Since the basic movements of ngo cho kun appear uncomplicated, many wrongly conclude that they are ineffective. The attacking techniques of ngo cho kun are powerful. Behind the simple movements lie strong, lethal strikes.

When moving, the ngo cho kun practitioner follows the principle of *semun,* or "four gates." This finds the practitioner moving in four directions, thereby developing a keen awareness of his surroundings. When attacking, the practitioner follows the "center-line" theory, and uses combination hand techniques to attack with continuous, pursuing steps, thereby crowding the opponent's defenses.

HAND TECHNIQUES

Since kung-fu is a pugilistic art, the hands play a principal role. Every style of kung-fu has its own unique hand techniques, some focusing on the fist, others utilizing the palms, fingers, wrist or any combination thereof. But whatever the movement, the hands are primarily used to deflect upward, thrust forward, hook downward, chop, strike, and grab, while extending or retracting.

The ngo cho kun practitioner who has mastered hand techniques becomes unpredictable in his movements. This occurs as a result of the constant interchange between offensive and defensive movements, or the combination of attack-block-attack. Movements may be either real or feints, the latter used to confuse an opponent and make him unable to determine the intention of your movements. This confusion will catch the opponent off-guard and allow the ngo cho kun practitioner to easily close the gap and deliver his intended blows. Having adequately completed the strength and conditioning training (*see* chaps. 13, 14), the ngo cho kun practitioner will attack the enemy with the idea that the torso is easier to hit than the head.

As a synthesis of five distinct kung-fu styles, ngo cho kun has techniques that deal with all aspects of hand-to-hand combat. The original 107 attacking hand techniques of ngo cho kun are listed in *The Complete Chinese Jujutsu*. Master Tan Ka Hong further increased the number of techniques to over 200 in his own "master text." Master Tan chose to illustrate examples of five categories of five techniques in his book: single short-hand techniques, single long-hand techniques, double short-hand techniques, double long-hand techniques, and kneeling-stance hand techniques. I have chosen to present these same movements here, thus offering a brief presentation of the twenty-five basic hand techniques of ngo cho kun.

Single Short-Hand Techniques

The five single short-hand techniques depicted here include the the whip strike, or backfist *(pian)*, which is delivered by striking down onto your opponent's nose with the back of your fist (Fig. 1); the uppercut *(kiao)*, which is delivered by striking up into your opponent's lower abdomen with your fist (Fig. 2); the hammer strike *(kong)*, which is delivered by striking down toward your opponent's chest with the back of your right fist (Fig. 3); the finger strike *(tok)*, which is delivered by thrusting your fingers vertically into your opponent's throat (Fig. 4); and the downward chop *(hong ko pua)*, which is delivered by striking down toward your opponent's neck with the knife-edge of your hand (Fig. 5).

Fig. 1   Fig. 2

Fig. 3

Fig. 4

Fig. 5

Fig. 6

Fig. 7

Single Long-Hand Techniques

The five single long-hand techniques depicted here include the straight punch *(tit chieng kun)*, which is delivered by holding the fist diagonally and punching straight from the waist toward your opponent's sternum (Fig. 6); the side straight chop *(tueh)*, which is delivered horizontally using the outside of the palm to strike your opponent's waist (Fig. 7); the slice chop *(chiat)*, which is delivered vertically using the outside of the palm to strike your opponent's waist (Fig. 8). The green-dragon-spot, or roundhouse punch *(chieng lieng tiam)*, which is delivered by swinging your arm and inverting your fist to strike your opponent's temple (Fig. 9); and the tiger claw *(ho liao)*, which is delivered vertically by thrusting your palm-heel into your opponent's chest (Fig. 10).

Fig. 8

Fig. 9

Fig. 10

Fig. 11

Fig. 12

Double Short-Hand Techniques

The five double short-hand techniques depicted here include the holding the sides strike *(po pian)*, which is delivered by striking to the side with both the palm of your left hand and side of your right fist (held in the phoenix-eye fist position) to your opponent's kidney (Fig. 11); the double uppercut *(sang kiao chiu)*, which is delivered upward into your opponent's abdomen with both fists (Fig. 12); the double penetrating uppercut *(sang kwan kun)*, which is delivered upward into your opponent's abdomen with both fists (the right arm more extended than the left) (Fig. 13); the hook uppercut *(kiao)*, which is delivered by simultaneously hooking your left hand and pulling it back toward your ribs while delivering an uppercut with your right fist into your opponent's abdomen (Fig. 14); the double closing scissors *(sang kwi chian)*, which is delivered by simultaneously closing your right and left arms together in front of your center-line (the left fist near your right elbow), thereby making a scissors action to break your opponent's arm (Fig. 15).

Fig. 13

Fig. 14

Fig. 15

Fig. 16

Fig. 17

Double Long-Hand Techniques

The five double long-hand techniques depicted here include the double green-dragon-spot *(sang lieng tiam taw)*, which is delivered by inverting your fists and swinging both arms to strike your opponent's temples (Fig. 16); the child-holding-the-tablet *(hi li po pai)*, which is delivered by holding both palms vertical and striking forward toward your opponent, so that the palm with fingers pointing up strikes the chest and the palm with fingers pointing down strikes the abdomen (Fig. 17); the double palm strike *(sang kwa chiu)*, which is delivered by holding both palms horizontally and striking forward toward your opponent's chest (Fig. 18); the double straight punch *(sang kiah kun)*, which is delivered by holding both fists vertically and punching forward to strike your opponent's chest (Fig. 19); and the double chop *(sang pueh)*, which is delivered by chambering both hands to one side (palms facing), then simultaneously chopping down with the bottom hand and across with the top hand, and sweeping with your left foot as you step forward to take down your opponent (Figs. 20, 21).

Fig. 18

Fig. 19

Fig. 20

Fig. 21

Fig. 22   Fig. 23

Fig. 24   Fig. 25   Fig. 26

Kneeling-Stance Hand Techniques

The five kneeling-stance hand techniques depicted here include the double palm strike *(sang tung chiu)*, which is delivered by dropping to one knee while striking forward with both palms (Fig. 22); the open bow snapping chop *(kwi kieng thua)*, which is delivered by turning sideways and dropping to one knee while snapping the outside of your palm horizontally toward your opponent (Fig. 23); the kneeling grab *(kut be so)*, which is delivered by dropping to one knee while simultaneously grabbing your opponent's arm with both hands (palms facing) (Figs. 24); the kneeling open-hand block *(kut be kay)*, which is delivered by dropping to one knee and snapping your open palm toward the ground to block your opponent's low strike or kick (Figs. 25); and the kneeling double-splitting block *(kut be sang li)*, which is delivered by dropping to one knee while spreading your right and left hands (palms down) toward their respective sides (one lower than the other), to block your opponent's double strike (Figs. 26).

LEG TECHNIQUES

Leg techniques play a secondary role in ngo cho kun, although they are no less effective. Leg techniques are generally relegated to the lower levels of an opponent's body. Kicks may be used as a distraction to help the practitioner enter into an opponent's space, or as a surprise maneuver following a hand technique combination. Sweeping maneuvers are primarily used to unbalance an opponent and set him up for a finishing blow. Take-down techniques are used as a reaction to being knocked to the ground, or when an opponent persists in kicking high and exposing his supporting leg. The following is a brief presentation of three basic leg techniques.

Cutting Hand Sweep

To deliver the cutting hand sweep *(sao kua chiu)* technique, chamber your right arm toward the left side of your face in preparation for a side chop (Fig. 27). Next, place your weight onto your left leg, and sweep forward with your right leg as you chop horizontally with the outside of your right palm (Fig. 28).

Fig. 27   Fig. 28

Fig. 29

Fig. 30

Fig. 31

Fig. 32

Continuous Cutting Hand Sweep

To deliver the continuous cutting-hand sweep *(lian kuan sao kua chiu)* technique, chamber your right arm toward the left side of your face in preparation for a side chop (Fig. 29). Next, place your weight onto your left leg, and sweep forward with your right leg as you chop horizontally with the outside of your right palm (Fig. 30). Again shift your weight onto your left leg as you simultaneously chamber your right arm for a tiger claw strike, and block outward with your left hand (Fig. 31). Follow-up by simultaneously sweeping your right foot backward (ending in a bow-and-arrow stance) and striking forward with a right-hand tiger claw (Fig. 32).

Fig. 33

Fig. 34

Fig. 35

Scissors Kick

To deliver the scissors kick *(puan chian wat)* technique, simultaneously bend your left knee to drop down while extending your right leg forward and blocking with your right hand (Fig. 33). Using the chambered force of your left leg, spring up and to the right, lifting your entire body into the air, while changing leg positions (Fig. 34). Finish by landing on your right side as your left leg kicks toward the right (Fig. 35).

6

Application of the Basics

INTRODUCTION

When engaged in a physical confrontation, the ngo cho kun practitioner draws his strength and ferocity from the five parts power *(ngo ki lat)*. The practitioner is then ready to engage his opponent in the center-arm on-guard position *(chi-ngo tiong ki)*, the classical fighting stance of ngo cho kun (Fig. 1). The following sections depict and describe the primary fighting application of the basic techniques of ngo cho kun.

Fig. 1

Fig. 2

Fig. 3

Fig. 4

HAND TECHNIQUES

Applying the Double Palm Strike

Face your opponent in the bow-and-arrow stance (Fig. 2). Step forward with your right foot and attempt a right-hand green-dragon-spot strike to your opponent's left temple, which he in turn blocks with his left arm while stepping back with his right leg (Fig. 3). You then step forward with your left leg and attempt a left-hand green-dragon-spot strike to your opponent's right temple, which he in turn blocks with his right arm while stepping back with his left leg (Fig. 4). As your opponent attempts to counter with a slice chop, you crowd him by stepping forward with your right foot, thus nullifying his strike (Fig. 5), and finish him off with a double palm strike to the chest (Figs. 6, 7).

Fig. 5

Fig. 6

Fig. 7

Fig. 8

Fig. 9

Applying the Tiger Claw

Engage your opponent in the classical center-arm on-guard position (Fig. 8). As your arms make contact, attack with a straight punch to your opponent's stomach, which he in turn blocks with his left arm (Fig. 9). With his block, the opponent has opened your center-line for a child-holding-the-tablet palm strike, which you simultaneously block and counter with a side straight chop (Figs. 10a, 10b). You immediately follow this by moving clockwise on your right foot to face the back of your opponent, and finish him off with a right-hand tiger claw strike (Fig. 11).

Fig. 10a

Fig. 10b

Fig. 11

Fig. 12

Fig. 13

Fig. 14

Fig. 15

Applying the Double Straight Punch

Face your opponent in a center-arm on-guard position while he faces you in a bow-and-arrow stance (Fig. 12). As your opponent shifts his stance and attacks with a straight punch, step slightly to the left while blocking downward with your right arm (Fig. 13). Immediately follow your right-arm block with a left-arm parry (Fig. 14). This opens your opponent's center-line which allows you to follow-up with a double straight punch, simultaneously striking his sternum and heart (Fig. 15).

Fig. 16

Fig. 17

Applying the Double Chop

You attack your opponent with a whip punch to the face, which he in turn blocks with his right forearm (Fig. 16). Upon impact, you simultaneously step forward with your right foot to sweep your opponent's lead leg, while striking his shoulder with your right forearm and his waist with your left forearm (Fig. 17).

Fig. 18

Fig. 19

Fig. 20

Applying the Kneeling Techniques

The following three photographs show the primary position of three kneeling-stance hand techniques: the open-bow snapping chop to the back of the knee of your opponent's lead leg (Fig. 18); the kneeling grab which is used to immobilize your opponent's attacking arm while pulling him off-balance and to the ground (Fig. 19); and the double splitting block which is used to block various types of double attacks, such as the double palm strike shown here (Fig. 20).

Fig. 21

Fig. 22

LEG TECHNIQUES

Applying the Cutting Kick

As your opponent attacks with a straight punch to your chest (Fig. 21), simultaneously block it with your right arm and deliver a right cutting kick to the shin of his lead leg (Fig. 22).

Fig. 23

Fig. 24

Applying the Continuous Cutting Hand Sweep

You and your opponent face-off in the bow-and-arrow stance (Fig. 23). Your opponent steps forward with his right leg and attempts to punch you with his right fist, which you in turn block with your right arm (Fig. 24). You then proceed to counter with a cutting hand sweep, which your opponent in turn evades by lifting his right leg and moving sideways (Fig. 25). Your opponent then places his right leg behind your right leg and counters with a right whip strike to your face, which you in turn block (Fig 26). You immediately follow this up by taking your opponent down with a simultaneous back sweep and tiger claw strike to his chest (Fig. 27).

Fig. 25

Fig. 26

Fig. 27

Fig. 28

Fig. 29

Fig. 30

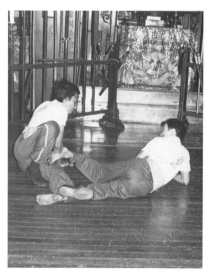

Fig. 31

Applying the Scissors Kick

Face your opponent in a natural fighting stance (Fig. 28). As your opponent initiates a front kick, step slightly to the right to evade it while lowering your stance by bending your left knee and extending your right leg forward (Fig. 29). Immediately upon evading, leap and change position, sliding your right leg to the side of your opponent's left leg, while chambering your left leg for a kick (Fig. 30). Take your opponent down by sweeping the outside of his left leg with your right leg and kicking the inside of his left knee with your left foot (Fig. 31).

PART THREE

Empty-Hand Forms of Ngo Cho Kun

7

Overview of the Forms

INTRODUCTION

Ngo cho kun kung-fu contains a wide variety of techniques which are learned through the practice of empty-hand forms. These forms increase in length, difficulty, and diversity as the student's training progresses and he advances through the system. Proficiency in ngo cho kun is gauged in part by the number of forms that a practitioner understands and can correctly perform. Correct delivery of the ordered movements consists of proper body positioning and smooth transitions from one technique to another, leading to the development of power.

As the nucleus of ngo cho kun, empty-hand forms are much revered by the masters. In fact, in times past, a masters would seldom teach the entire set of movements which comprise a form to his students. Malaysian ngo cho kun master, Yap Ching Hai, stated in his book, *Ngo Cho Kun To Swat* (Ngo Cho Kun Illustrated), that once when he performed the *sam chien* form in front of an old master's students, this master told him that the form is very secretive and should not be shown to beginners. In kung-fu there is a saying: *"Ge put twan liok he"* (Don't teach the art if there are six ears around). In other words, since a man has two ears, if there are three people present the secrets must not be revealed.

CLASSIFICATION OF THE FORMS

The forms of ngo cho kun are classified as either *chien* (tension) or *kun* (fist). Compared with the majority of forms found in other systems of kung-fu, those found in ngo cho kun are relatively short, and stripped of flowery movements, thus tending to be more efficient and practical.

There are ten *chien* forms which serve as a means of increasing the practitioner's power and strength. During the execution of the form's movements tension and breath are combined to strengthen the body. If properly trained, this combination simultaneously develops the iron-vest

73

body *(ti po sha)*, which enables the practitioner to withstand the receipt of a powerful blow, and increases one's striking power by integrating the five parts power into the form.

Traditionally, students were not taught the *kun* forms if they had not yet developed sufficient power in their *chien* forms. The most common *kun* form is *li sip kun* (twenty punches fist), wherein students are taught how to punch correctly, with coordination and power. *Kun* forms are not performed with the tension of the *chien* forms, but with sharp, swift movement combinations. Sifu Tan Ka Hong used to say: *"Lien kun pi se."* Roughly translated, this means that when practicing the *kun* forms, one should merely perform the posture or techniques where strength and rhythm comes without great effort. This, of course, only occurs if one has properly trained in the *chien* forms.

Ngo cho kun has more than forty empty-hand forms (*see* Appendix 1). Within these forms are techniques suited for different physiques. The burly man, for instance, can practice hard techniques, while the small man can concentrate on defensive forms and in the development of speed, with special attention given to those techniques used for attacking the lower extremities. Ngo cho kun also has soft forms suitable for women and the elderly, such as its *ho chien wat* (crane), *chieng hong* (cool breeze), and *pe guan chu tong* (monkey) forms. Thus, ngo cho kun is an art suited for everyone regardless of body-type, gender, or age. In this book, I have chosen the *sam chien* and *in tin tat* forms, which are *chien* and *kun* forms respectively, to offer the reader a sample of the ngo cho kun forms. In addition, I have included the basic application of the forms' movements, to offer the reader a clearer understanding of the intended purpose of each movement.

OPENING AND CLOSING THE FORMS

All ngo cho kun forms open with the same combination of movements, known as the *qi kun*, or opening fist. The opening fist is comprised of a sequence of five distinct movements.

The first movement is called *ti tui tim kang* (metal hammer sinking in the river). To begin, stand in the level horse stance and clench your fists (Fig. 1). Next, using dynamic tension, slowly pull your hands to the sides of your torso (Fig. 2).

Fig. 1   Fig. 2

The second movement is called *kim chian tuat kock* (golden cicada shedding its skin). Continue by opening your fists, so that your palms face the floor and your fingers point toward one another, as you thrust your hands downward (Fig. 3).

The third movement is called *bi lin sue cheng* (the lady-fixing-her-hair). Continue by swinging both hands upward, crossing them in front of your body along the way, and separate them outward at eyebrow level, with the fingers of both hands pointing outward (Fig. 4).

The forth movement is called *Kwan Peng po in* (General Kwan Peng holding the seal). Continue by simultaneously pulling your right fist back to the right side of your ribs while moving your left palm toward your right fist, covering it (Fig. 5). Slowly stretch your right fist and left palm, held together, forward in front of your chest forming the traditional kung-fu bow, which means "everywhere all men are equal" (Fig. 6).

The fifth movement is called *sang lieng chiu tsu* (double dragon fighting for the pearl). Continue by releasing the contact between your hands and, with palms facing up, and slowly twist your torso to the right while pulling your hands to their respective sides, at chest level (Fig. 7). Next, bring your palms forward using tension, and twist the upper torso to the starting frontal position. Lower your hands with palms facing out (Fig. 8).

Fig. 3

Fig. 4

Fig. 5

Fig. 6

Fig. 7

Fig. 8

Fig. 9   Fig. 10

All ngo cho kun forms end in one of two closing fist *(siu kun)* postures. The *chien* forms end in the *siu po pai* (shield-holding hand) posture (Fig. 9), a final tension movement and finishing strike. The *kun* forms end in the *chiao yung chiu* (enticing hand) posture (Fig. 10), an on-guard stance assumed after a final blow in anticipation of another attack.

8

The Sam Chien Tension Form

INTRODUCTION

The *sam chien* (three wars) form is the foundation of ngo cho kun. While its movements may appear uncomplicated, do not be deceived. Within the framework of this form are the fundamental movements upon which the nucleus of all ngo cho kun techniques are derived. In fact, within its movements are found the four attributes that govern the entire ngo cho kun system: float, sink, swallow, and spit out. *Pu* (float) is an attack that forces an opponent off balance, making him feel as if he is treading on water. *Tim* (sink) controls the opponent's movement, making him feel as if he were carrying a heavy weight. *Tun* (swallow) deflects a strike so that it misses its intended target. *Tu* (spit out) is a powerful push used to send the opponent away.

Indeed, *sam chien* is recognized as the most basic—and most advanced—form in ngo cho kun. To understand this, the practitioner has to delve deep into his studies and persevere in his training to fully comprehend the movements. Perhaps after several years of dedicated practice and study, the student will at last come to comprehend that all techniques spring from this fundamental form. As Sifu Tan Ka Hong used to state: "The wonders of ngo cho kun are found inside the *sam chien*."

For the average practitioner, it takes about eight months of hard training to develop the proper stance, perfect the physical movements, cultivate the five parts power *(ngo ki lat)*, and circulate the intrinsic energy *(ching)*. In a nutshell, *sam chien* is the internal energy *(chi kung)* and iron body *(ti po sha)* exercise of ngo cho kun. Diligent and prolonged practice of *sam chien* develops patience and strength, and produces a strong body that yields dynamic strength and intrinsic energy.

The *sam chien* form is performed in three parts: the *qi kun*, or opening fist, which serves as the bow or salutation of all the ngo cho kun forms; the *sam chien* form itself; and the *siu po pai*, or closing fist, which ends all

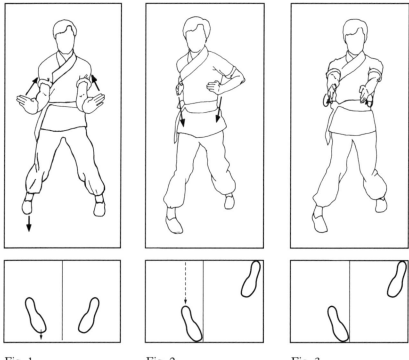

Fig. 1   Fig. 2   Fig. 3

of the tension forms. The physical movements of the *sam chien* form are few. Three steps are taken forward and three backward while maintaining a fighting *chien be* stance. With each step, the arms thrust forward, drop down, curl in, and push forward into a ready position. An arm break, low block, elbow strike, palm technique, and sweeping block follow to end the form.

DESCRIPTION OF THE FORM

1. Sang Lieng Chiu Tsu (Double Dragon Fighting for the Pearl)

Prior to starting the form, be sure to complete the entire opening fist set (*see* chap. 7). Begin the *sam chien* form from the last movement of the opening fist (Fig. 1).

2. Tit Chin Po, Sang Cha (Forward Step, Double Finger Thrust)

Step forward with your right leg into a *chien be* stance, and pull both arms backward until your palms are at the sides of your ribs while inhaling through your nose (Fig. 2). Next, thrust your hands forward and slightly down, focusing your strength on your fingertips, while letting out a short exhalation of breath through your mouth (Fig. 3). The whole body should be tensed.

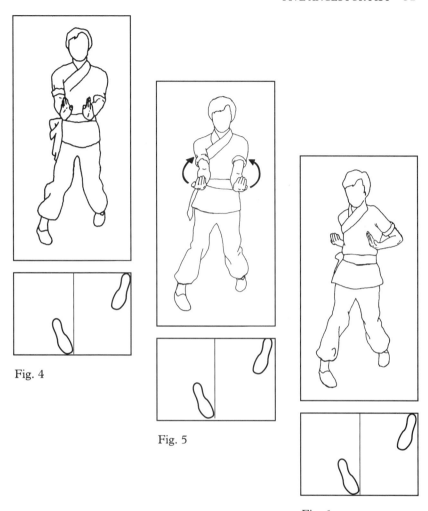

Fig. 4

Fig. 5

Fig. 6

3. Che Chat (Bending the Joint)

Slowly bend your elbows while stretching your fingers toward the ceiling and sucking in your shoulders (Fig. 4). Continue exhaling through your mouth, while maintaining tension in your body.

4. Tun Chiu (Swallowing the Hand)

Slowly turn your palms outward until your palms face the ceiling (Fig. 5). Then, while inhaling through the nose and turning your torso sideways, tense and slowly retract your arms, palms facing up, until they reach their respective sides of your torso (Fig. 6).

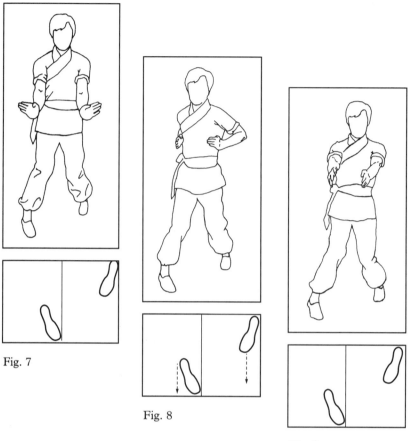

Fig. 7

Fig. 8

Fig. 9

5. Chun Chiu (Vibrating the Hand)

Next, tense your stomach muscles as you focus strength in your arms and push them out and down to waist level (Fig. 7). You should exhale through your mouth and exert strength as you push your arms out until you feel them vibrate. You have now returned to the final position of the opening fist set.

6. Tit Chin Po, Sang Cha (Forward Step, Double Finger Thrust)

Step forward five inches with your right leg, moving into a *chien be* stance. Pull both arms back until your palms are at the sides of your ribs while inhaling through your nose (Fig. 8). Next, thrust your hands forward and slightly down, focusing your strength on your fingertips, while letting out a short exhalation of breath through your mouth (Fig. 9). The whole body should be tensed.

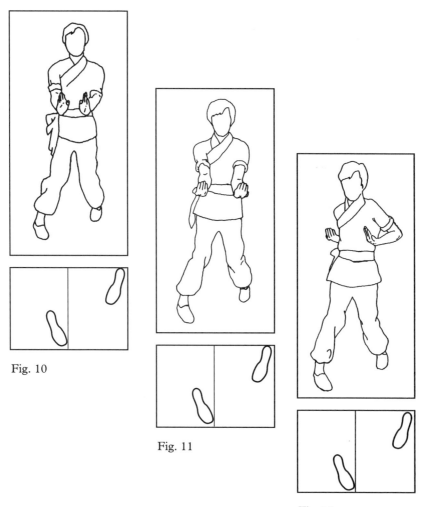

Fig. 10

Fig. 11

Fig. 12

7. *Che Chat (Bending the Joint)*

Slowly bend your elbows while stretching your fingers toward the ceiling and sucking in your shoulders (Fig. 10). Continue exhaling through your mouth, while maintaining tension in your body.

8. *Tun Chiu (Swallowing the Hand)*

Slowly turn your palms outward until your palms face the ceiling (Fig. 11). Then, while inhaling through the nose and turning your torso sideways, tense and slowly retract your arms, palms facing up, until they reach their respectice sides of your torso (Fig. 12).

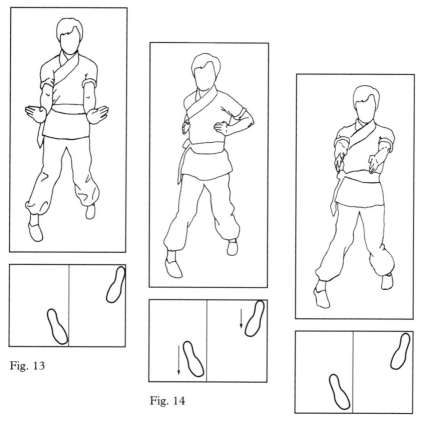

Fig. 13

Fig. 14

Fig. 15

9. Chun Chiu (Vibrating the Hand)

Next, tense your stomach muscles as you focus strength in your arms and push them out and down to waist level (Fig. 13). You should exhale through your mouth and exert strength as you push your arms out until you feel them vibrate. You have now returned to the final position of the opening fist set.

10. Tit Chin Po, Sang Cha (Forward Step, Double Finger Thrust)

Step forward five inches with your right leg, moving into a *chien be* stance. Pull both arms back until your palms are at the sides of your ribs while inhaling through your nose (Fig. 14). Next, thrust your hands forward and slightly down, focusing your strength on your fingertips, while letting out a short exhalation of breath through your mouth (Fig. 15). The whole body should be tensed.

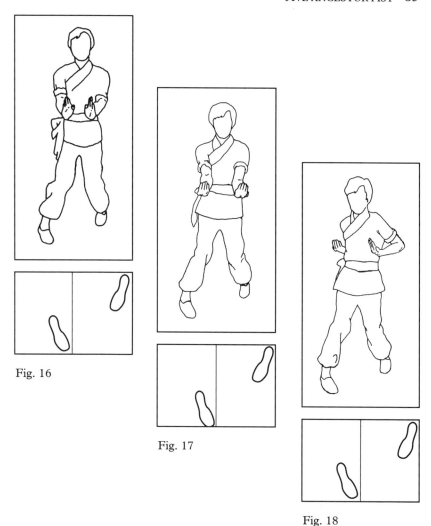

Fig. 16

Fig. 17

Fig. 18

11. Che Chat (Bending the Joint)

Slowly bend your elbows while stretching your fingers toward the ceiling and sucking in your shoulders (Fig. 16). Continue exhaling through your mouth, while maintaining tension in your body.

12. Tun Chiu (Swallowing the Hand)

Slowly turn your palms outward until your palms face the ceiling (Fig. 17). Then, while inhaling through the nose and turning your torso sideways, tense and slowly retract your arms, palms facing up, until they reach their respectice sides of your torso (Fig. 18).

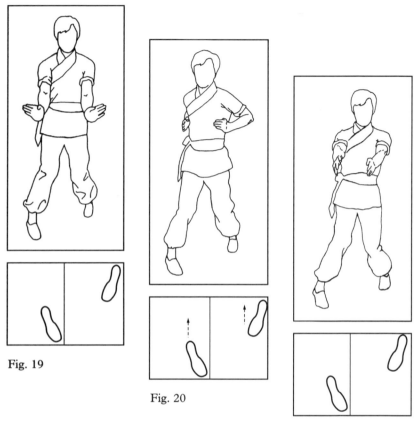

Fig. 19

Fig. 20

Fig. 21

13. Chun Chiu (Vibrating the Hand)

Next, tense your stomach muscles as you focus strength in your arms and push them out and down to waist level (Fig. 19). You should exhale through your mouth and exert strength as you push your arms out until you feel them vibrate. You have now returned to the final position of the opening fist set.

14. Tit Te Po, Sang Cha (Backward Step, Double Finger Thrust)

Step backward five inches with your right leg, moving into a *chien be* stance. Pull both arms back until your palms are at the sides of your ribs while inhaling through your nose (Fig. 20). Next, thrust your hands forward and slightly down, focusing your strength on your fingertips, while letting out a short exhalation of breath through your mouth (Fig. 21). The whole body should be tensed.

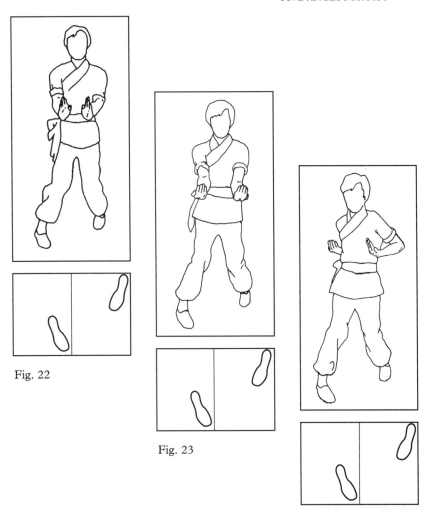

Fig. 22

Fig. 23

Fig. 24

15. Che Chat (Bending the Joint)

Slowly bend your elbows while stretching your fingers toward the ceiling and sucking in your shoulders (Fig. 22). Continue exhaling through your mouth, while maintaining tension in your body.

16. Tun Chiu (Swallowing the Hand)

Slowly turn your palms outward until your palms face the ceiling (Fig. 23). Then, while inhaling through the nose and turning your torso sideways, tense and slowly retract your arms, palms facing up, until they reach their respectice sides of your torso (Fig. 24).

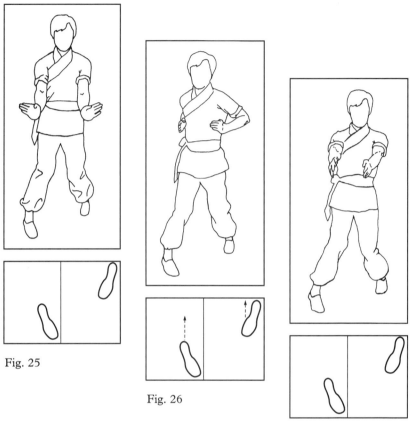

Fig. 25

Fig. 26

Fig. 27

17. Chun Chiu (Vibrating the Hand)

Next, tense your stomach muscles as you focus strength in your arms and push them out and down to waist level (Fig. 25). You should exhale through your mouth and exert strength as you push your arms out until you feel them vibrate. You have now returned to the final position of the opening fist set.

18. Tit Te Po, Sang Cha (Backward Step, Double Finger Thrust)

Step backward five inches with your right leg, moving into a *chien be* stance. Pull both arms back until your palms are at the sides of your ribs while inhaling through your nose (Fig. 26). Next, thrust your hands forward and slightly down, focusing your strength on your fingertips, while letting out a short exhalation of breath through your mouth (Fig. 27). The whole body should be tensed.

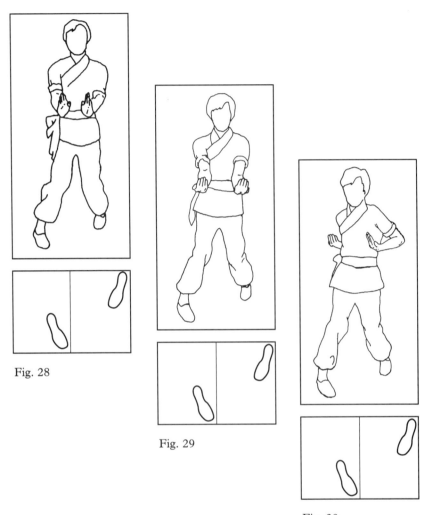

Fig. 28

Fig. 29

Fig. 30

19. Che Chat (Bending the Joint)

Slowly bend your elbows while stretching your fingers toward the ceiling and sucking in your shoulders (Fig. 28). Continue exhaling through your mouth, while maintaining tension in your body.

20. Tun Chiu (Swallowing the Hand)

Slowly turn your palms outward until your palms face the ceiling (Fig. 29). Then, while inhaling through the nose and turning your torso sideways, tense and slowly retract your arms, palms facing up, until they reach their respectice sides of your torso (Fig. 30).

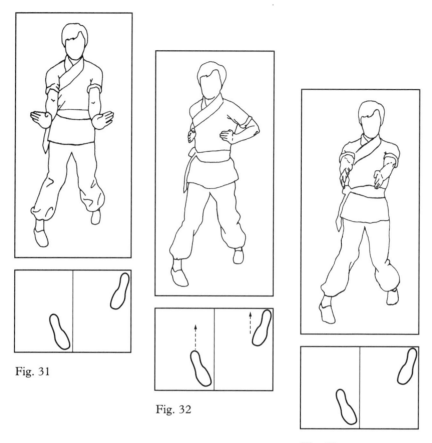

Fig. 31

Fig. 32

Fig. 33

21. Chun Chiu (Vibrating the Hand)

Next, tense your stomach muscles as you focus strength in your arms and push them out and down to waist level (Fig. 31). You should exhale through your mouth and exert strength as you push your arms out until you feel them vibrate. You have now returned to the final position of the opening fist set.

22. Tit Te Po, Sang Cha (Backward Step, Double Finger Thrust)

Step backward five inches with your right leg into a *chien be* stance, and pull both arms back until your palms are at the sides of your ribs while inhaling through your nose (Fig. 32). Next, thrust your hands forward and slightly down, focusing your strength on your fingertips, while letting out a short exhalation of breath through your mouth (Fig. 33). The whole body should be tensed.

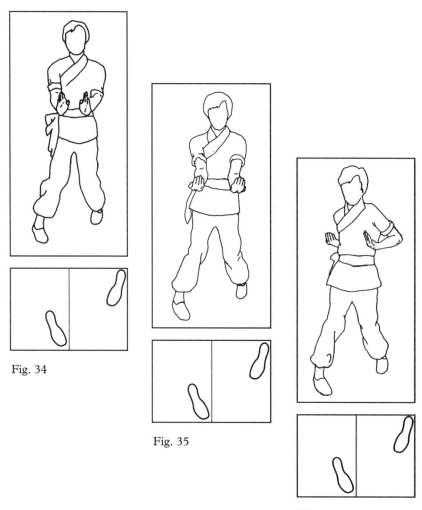

Fig. 34

Fig. 35

Fig. 36

23. Che Chat (Bending the Joint)

Slowly bend your elbows while stretching your fingers toward the ceiling and sucking in your shoulders (Fig. 34). Continue exhaling through your mouth, while maintaining tension in your body.

24. Tun Chiu (Swallowing the Hand)

Slowly turn your palms outward until your palms face the ceiling (Fig. 35). Then, while inhaling through the nose and turning your torso sideways, tense and slowly retract your arms, palms facing up, until they reach their respectice sides of your torso (Fig. 36).

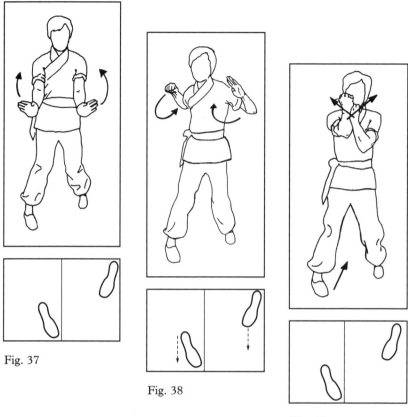

Fig. 37

Fig. 38

Fig. 39

25. Chun Chiu (Vibrating the Hand)

Next, tense your stomach muscles as you focus strength in your arms and push them out and down to waist level (Fig. 37). You should exhale through your mouth and exert strength as you push your arms out until you feel them vibrate. You have now returned to the final position of the opening fist set.

26. Tit Chin Sang Kue Chian (Double Scissors Block)

Without moving your stance, chamber your arms to the sides of their respective shoulders, with the right fist clenched and the left hand open (Fig. 38). Next, Step forward five inches with first your right leg and then your left, maintaining the proper *chien be* stance. While stepping, simultaneously close your right and left arms together in front of your center-line (the left fist near your right elbow), thereby simulating a scissors action (Fig. 39).

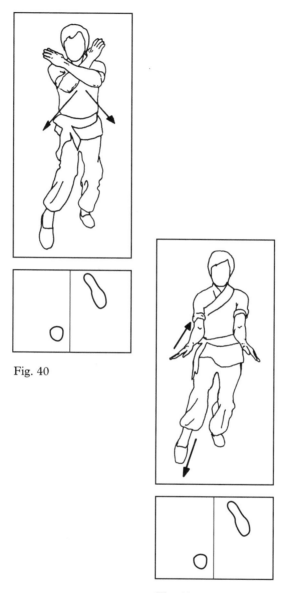

Fig. 40

Fig. 41

27. *Te Kia Sang Kaw (Hanging Leg Stance, Double Hook Block)*

Step back with your left leg into a hanging-leg stance while crossing
your arms at chest level (Fig. 40). Next, swing your arms down to stomach level, with your elbows tucked in at the sides of your stomach and
your fingers pointing down and slightly out (Fig. 41).

Fig. 42

Fig. 43

Fig. 44

28. Tit Chin Po, Pa Chat (Forward Step, Elbow Strike)

Step forward five inches with your right leg into a *chien be* stance. While stepping, chamber your right arm, fist clenched, to the right side of your body while maintaining the position of your left hand (Fig. 42). Next, strike horizontally with your right elbow into your left palm (Fig. 43).

29. Peng Yu Chiu Sia (Side Chop)

Retract your left hand back to its respective side while chopping horizontally forward with your right palm (Fig. 44).

Fig. 45

Fig. 46

30. Cho Chiu Chiat (Slice Chop)

Retract your right hand to its respective side while thrusting vertically forward with the palm of your left hand (Fig. 45).

31. Yu Chiu Tue (Straight Side Thrust)

To complete the form, retract your left hand to the left side of your torso, thrusting horizontally forward with your right hand (Fig. 46).

Siu kun (closing Fist)

Now that the movements of the sam chien form are finished, assume the *sui po pai* closing fist posture. To do this, step back with your left leg into a right hanging-leg stance, push your right and left palms out slowly until they are in front of you, with the position of both hands parallel to your center (*see* chap. 7).

APPLICATION OF THE FORM

As stated earlier, *sam chien* is a form primarily used to strengthen and condition the body. It is an isotonic exercise used to enhance the endurance of the body, the stability of stances and blocks, and the power of strikes. However, its final series of movements contain fighting techniques proper. Following are examples of the primary application of those techniques.

Applying the Double Closing Scissors Technique (Figs. 38, 39 in the Form)

As your opponent attacks with a left straight punch, block and grab his arm with your left hand (Fig. 1). Immediately follow this up by twisting your opponent's wrist counterclockwise and slamming your right forearm into the back of his elbow joint, breaking his arm (Fig. 2).

Fig. 1

Fig. 2

Fig. 3

Fig. 4

Applying the Double Hook Block (Figs. 40, 41 in the Form)

As your opponent attacks you with a double uppercut strike, step back into a hanging-leg stance and block the strike with the double hook block (Fig. 3). You may follow this up with a front groin kick, should you so desire (Fig. 4).

Fig. 5

Fig. 6

Fig. 7

Applying the Elbow Strike (Figs. 42, 43 in the Form)

As your opponent attacks with a right straight punch, block and grab his forearm with your left hand (Fig. 5). Upon seizing his forearm immediately move his arm to the left and step your right leg behind his lead leg as you prepare to strike his chest with your right elbow (Fig. 6). Take your opponent down by simultaneously striking his chest with your right elbow and sweeping his right leg with the backward motion of your right leg (Fig. 7).

Fig. 8

Fig. 9

Fig. 10

Fig. 11

Applying the Side Chop, Palm Chop, Side Thrust (Figs. 43–46 in the Form)

If your opponent blocks your right elbow strike (previous technique) by stepping back with his right leg and raising his right forearm (Fig. 8), parry his right hand with your left hand and chamber your right by your left shoulder (Fig. 9). From this position, deliver three consecutive strikes: a right side chop to your opponent's neck (Fig. 10), a left straight

Fig. 12

Fig. 13

palm chop to his waist (Fig. 11), and a right straight side thrust to his chest (Fig. 12).

Applying the Shield Holding Hand, 1 (Closing Fist)

As your opponent attacks with a right straight punch, thrust forward with a left palm to at once deflect his punching arm and strike his face, while your right palm strikes his stomach, and your front kick strikes his groin (Fig. 13).

Fig. 14

Fig. 15

Fig. 16

Applying the Shield Holding Hand, 2 (Closing Fist)

As your opponent attacks with a right straight punch, raise and extend your right arm to block (Fig. 14). Immediately upon impact, grab and twist your opponent's wrist clockwise with your right hand, while pushing on his elbow with your left hand (Fig. 15). While maintaining the arm-bar hold, kick your opponent in the groin with a right front kick (Fig. 16).

9

The In Tin Tat Fist Form

INTRODUCTION

Since *in tin tat* is one of ngo cho kun's more complicated forms it is reserved for the advanced student. Training in this form acquaints the practitioner with complex methods of body shifting and side stepping in addition to various kicking, striking, grappling, and ground fighting techniques.

In tin tat teaches the practitioner various fighting skills. Examples include the front kick, palm strike, and double penetrating uppercut combination; the entwining grab, throw, and arm break combination; the inverted punch used to counter when you have been grabbed by an opponent; and the follow-up kick used as a response to an opponent who has nullified your grabbing techniques. In addition, this form introduces the lotus stance, which serves as a transition movement to facilitate immediate ground fighting from a standing position.

In essence, the *in tin tat* form exposes the student to a diversity of practical fighting techniques. In addition, this form may be practiced with a partner as a two-man set to further enhance proper execution of the ordered movements in an actual physical confrontation. The form must be practiced diligently, until the techniques become reflexive and natural.

DESCRIPTION OF THE FORM

1. Sang Lieng Chiu Tsu (Double Dragon Fighting for the Pearl)

Prior to starting the form be sure to complete the entire opening fist set (*see* chap. 7) Begin the *in tin tat* form from the last movement of the opening fist (Fig. 1).

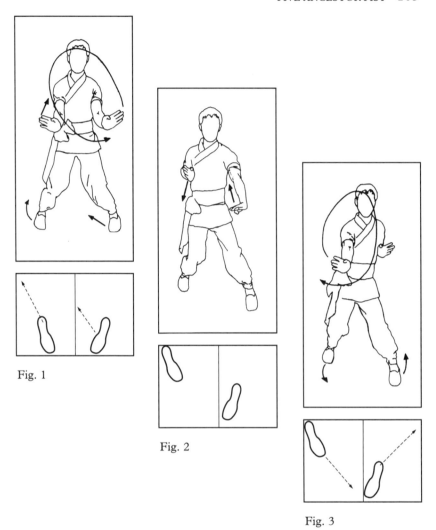

Fig. 1

Fig. 2

Fig. 3

2. Siam Yu Puan, Cho Chiu Kai (Evade Right, Left Downward Block)

Shift to the right by stepping back with your right leg and then your left, ending in a left *chien be* stance, while simultaneously executing a left open hand downward block (Fig. 2).

3. Yu Chiu Chiat (Slice Chop)

Retract your left hand to the left side of your torso while simultaneously striking forward with a right hand slice chop (Fig. 3).

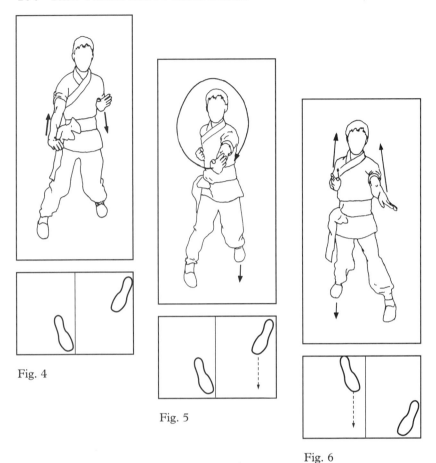

Fig. 4

Fig. 5

Fig. 6

4. Siam Cho Puan, Yu Chiu Kai (Evade Left, Right Downward Block)

Shift to the left by stepping back with your left leg and then your right, ending in a right *chien be* stance, while simultaneously executing a right open hand downward block (Fig. 4).

5. Cho Chiu Chiat (Slice Chop)

Retract your right hand to the right side of your torso while executing a left slice chop (Fig. 5).

6. Uwa Cho Chiok, Cho Chiu Kim (Forward Step, Grabbing Block)

Step forward with your left leg into a left *chien be* stance and execute a left grabbing block by swinging your left hand counterclockwise (Fig. 6).

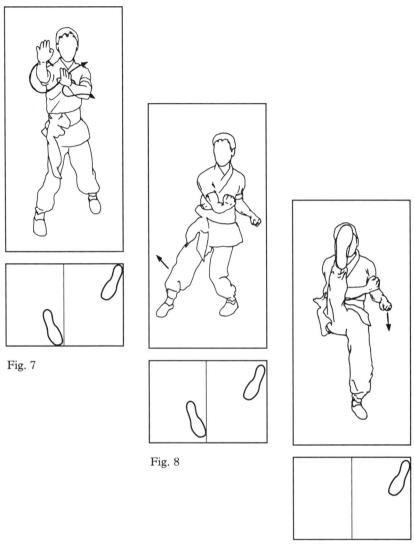

Fig. 7

Fig. 8

Fig. 9

7. *Ta Yu Chiok, In Tin So, Yu Chiok Tat (Forward Step, Entwining Grab, Front Kick)*

Step forward with your right leg into a right *chien be* stance, while extending both hands forward in preparation to grab your opponent's hand (Fig. 7). Abruptly retract both hands to the left side of your torso with the left fist facing downward and the right fist facing upward (Fig. 8). Deliver a front kick with your right foot (Fig. 9).

Fig. 10

Fig. 11

Fig. 12

8. Cho Chiat, Yu Chiu Tue(Slice Chop, Straight Side Thrust Chop)

Step down with your right foot in a right *chien be* stance and execute a left slice chop (Fig. 10). Retract your left hand to the left side of your torso and execute a right straight chop (Fig. 11).

9. Tit Chin Sang Kwan Tiong Kun(Forward Step, Double Penetrating Uppercut)

Step forward with your right leg, and then your left, while clenching both fists as you bring them down to your sides (Fig. 12). Immediately

Fig. 13

Fig. 14

Fig. 15

follow this by swinging both fists upward to execute a double penetrating uppercut (Fig. 13).

10. Te Yu Chiok Hiong Yu Puan, Sang Kai Sua (Retreating Step, Double Open line Block)

Swing your right leg back, turn toward the right, shifting your left foot toward your right foot (assuming a level horse stance), while simultaneously executing a double open-line block (with both hands in the phoenix-eye fist position) by swinging both hands up and to the side of your body (Fig. 14). (Front view, Fig. 15).

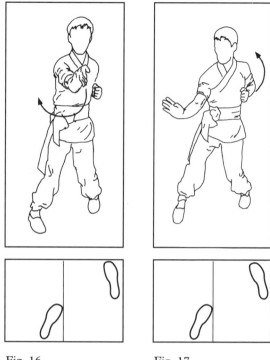

Fig. 16   Fig. 17

11. Hwan Aw Yu Chiu Tok (Back Pivot, Finger Strike)

Turn to your right by first moving your left leg to the right and stepping forward with your right leg into a right *chien be* stance, while executing a right finger strike (Fig. 16).

12. Peng Kay, Cho Chiu Pian(Scooping Block, Whip Punch)

Execute a right scooping block by swinging your right arm counterclockwise (Fig. 17). Chamber your left fist behind your head and strike down with a left whip punch (Figs. 18, 19).

13. Uwa Cho Chiok, Cho Chiu Tok (Shift to Left Leg, Finger strike)

Shift stances by stepping back with your right leg and forward with your left leg into a left *chien be* stance, while executing a left finger strike (Fig. 20).

14. Peng Kay, Yu Chiu Pian (Scooping Block, Whip Punch)

Execute a left scooping block by swinging your left arm counterclockwise (Fig. 21). Chamber your right fist behind your head and strike down with a right whip punch (Figs. 22, 23).

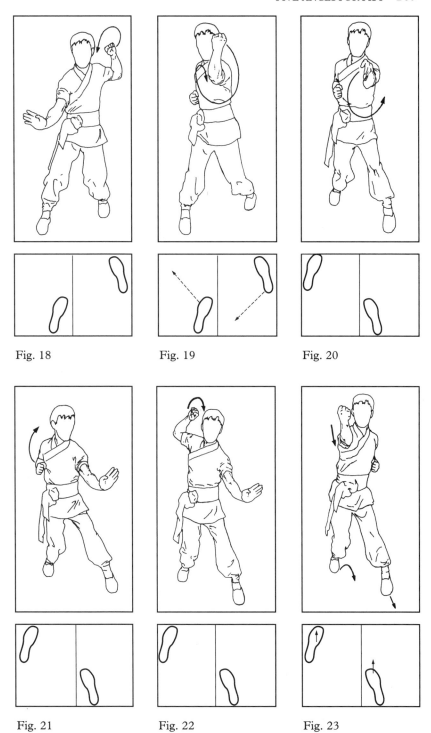

Fig. 18

Fig. 19

Fig. 20

Fig. 21

Fig. 22

Fig. 23

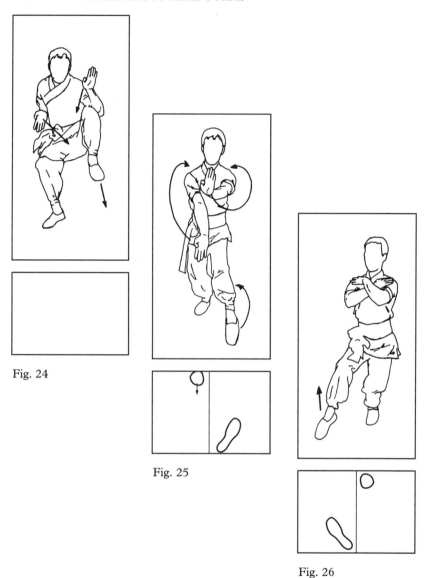

Fig. 24

Fig. 25

Fig. 26

15. Tiao Chin, Hay Li Po Pai (Forward Jump, Palm Strike)

Jump forward with your right leg into a right hanging-leg stance and execute a children holding the tablet palm strike (Figs. 24, 25).

16. Tiao Te Aw, Sang Tze Hieng, Peng Tat (Jump Backward, Cross Hand Block, Front Kick)

Jump backward with your right leg into a left hanging-leg stance, while

Fig. 27

Fig. 28

Fig. 29

performing a cross-hand covering block (Fig. 26). Raise your right knee (Fig. 27) and execute a front kick (Fig. 28).

17. Tap Che Lian Hiong Yu (Retreat Into Lotus Posture)

Step backward with your right leg as your left leg moves behind it assuming a cross-stance, while turning your palms so that they face outward (Fig. 29).

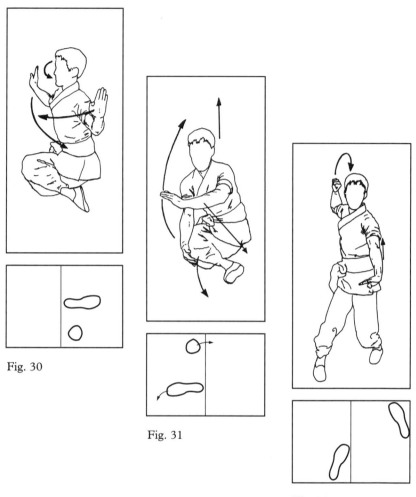

Fig. 30

Fig. 31

Fig. 32

18. Tsuan Hiong Aw, Lek Si Tun (Body Turn, Ground Grabbing Technique)

Kneel down with your crossed legs to assume a lotus stance, while chopping down and out with both palms (Fig. 30). Shift your upper torso to your left, extend your right palm forward with your left palm pushing down, while pulling back with your right hand, performing the ground grabbing techniques (Fig. 31).

19 & 20. Ta Yu Chiok, Yu Chiu Kong (Forward Step, Hammer Strike)

Stand up into a right *chien be* stance, chamber your right hand to the

Fig. 33

Fig. 34

Fig. 35

right side of your head, and execute a left hand open-hand downward block (Fig. 32). Retract your left hand to its respective side and deliver a hammer strike with your right hand (Fig. 33).

21. Peng Tioh (Outside Block)

Pivot your right arm clockwise and execute a right open-hand outside block (Fig. 34).

22. Cho Chiu Chiat (Slice Chop)

Retract your right hand to its respective side while executing a left slice chop (Fig. 35).

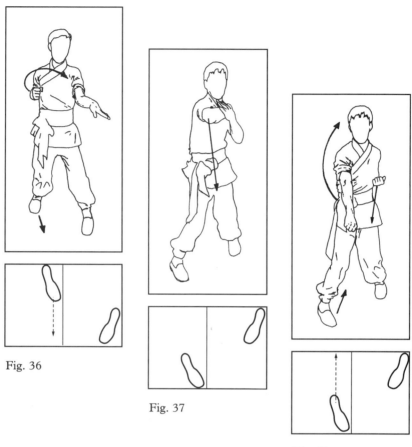

Fig. 36

Fig. 37

Fig. 38

23. Hwan Chiu, Ta Yu Giok, Cho Chiu Kim (Frontal Pivot, Step, Crossing Block)

Pivot 180-degrees to the left (so that you once again face forward) by stepping toward your left with your right leg, then turning your left leg so that you assume a left *chien be* stance. Execute a left grabbing block (Fig. 36).

24. Yu Chiu Pa Chat (Elbow Strike)

Step forward with your right leg into a right *chien be* stance while executing a right elbow strike into your left palm (Fig. 37).

25. Peng Wan Tui (Inverted Punch)

From this position, execute a right inverted punch by striking downward with your right fist (Fig. 38). Step back with your left leg into a left

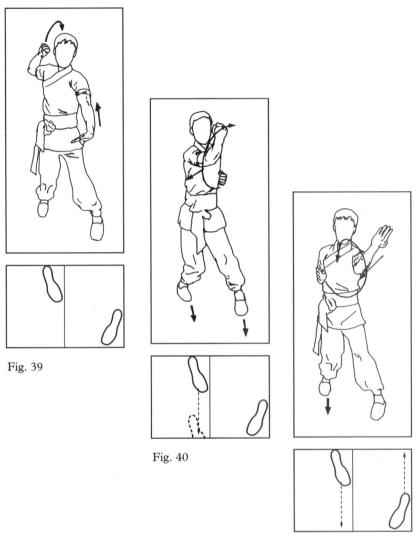

Fig. 39

Fig. 40

Fig. 41

chien be stance, push down with your left hand, and chamber your right hand next to your ear (Fig. 39). From this position, strike down with a right whip punch while retracting your left hand (Fig. 40).

26. Tiap Chin Cho Chiok, Cho Chiu Tioh (Double Forward Step, Outside Block)

Step forward with your right foot and then your left foot into a left *chien be* stance, and execute a left open-hand outside block (Fig. 41).

Fig.42

27. Uwa Be Yu Chiok, Yu Chiu Hongko Piak (Shift Stance, Downward Chop)

Change stance by stepping back with your left leg and then step forward with your right leg while executing a right downward chop with your right hand (Fig. 42).

Chiao Yong Chiu (Closing Fist)

Now that the movements of the *in tin tat* form are finished, assume the *chiao yong chiu* closing fist posture. To do this, step back into a right hanging-leg stance and raise your palms in a clenched fist to ear level, bringing both hands to the center, with the right palm at nose level, the left palm close behind it (*see* chap. 7).

APPLICATION OF THE FORM

Since *in tin tat* is not a tension form but a fist form, its movements are designed expressly for use in hand-to-hand combat. As such, the practical applications of this form are many and diverse. Following are examples of the primary applications of the *in tin tat* fist form.

Fig. 1

Fig. 2

Fig. 3

Fig. 4

Applying the Downward Block, Slice Chop (Figs. 2–5 in the Form)

As your opponent attacks with a left center punch, shift your body to the right as you block with a left open-hand downward block (Fig. 1), and counter with a left slice chop to your opponent's ribs (Fig. 2). Your opponent then attacks with a right center punch, which you in turn block with a right open-hand downward block (Fig. 3), and counter with a left slice chop to your opponent's ribs (Fig. 4).

Fig. 5

Fig. 6

Fig. 7

Fig. 8

Applying the Grabbing Block, Entwining Grab, Entwining Kick (Figs. 6–9 in the Form)

As your opponent attacks with a right center punch, simultaneously block and grab his inner elbow with your left hand (Fig. 5). Your opponent follows this up by attacking with a left center punch, which you defend against by simultaneously using your right hand to grab his bicep and your left hand to grab his wrist (Fig. 6). As you attempt to pull your opponent off balance and to the ground, he counters by abruptly retracting his left arm and striking your right arm with his right arm (Fig. 7).

Fig. 9

Fig. 10

Not wanting to lose the advantage of the situation, release your hold and kick your opponent with a right front groin kick (Fig. 8).

Applying the Double Penetrating Uppercut (Figs. 12, 13 in the Form)

As your opponent attacks with a right center punch, counter with a right closed-hand downward block (Fig. 9). Immediately follow this action by countering with a double penetrating uppercut, with your right fist striking his chin and your left fist striking his sternum (Fig. 10).

Fig. 11

Fig. 12

Applying the Open Line Block (Fig. 14 in the Form)

As your opponent attacks with a double hook punch, block by thrusting both of your hands outward, with hands held in a phoenix-eye fist position, curled upward to tense the forearm (Fig. 11).

Applying the Finger Strike (Fig. 16 in the Form)

As your opponent attacks with a right punch, counter by simultaneously blocking the punch with your right forearm and striking your opponent in the deltoid or throat with a finger strike (Fig. 12).

Fig. 13

Fig. 14

Applying the Scooping Block, Whip Punch (Figs. 17–20 in the Form)

As your opponent attacks with a right uppercut, block it with a right-hand scooping block by swinging your right arm counterclockwise, thereby sliding under your opponent's attacking arm (Fig. 13). Follow this up by locking your opponent's arm by hooking your wrist around his wrist, pulling it toward you to immobilize it, and striking your opponent's face with a whip punch (Fig. 14).

Fig. 15

Fig. 16

Fig. 17

Applying the Child-Holding-the-Tablet Palm Strike (Fig. 24, 25 in the Form)

As your opponent prepares for an attack, or upon finding an opening in his defenses, immediately jump forward into a right hanging-leg stance and strike your opponent vertically with both palms, simultaneously striking his face and ribs (Fig. 15).

Applying the Cross-Hand Covering Block, Front Kick (Figs. 26–28 in the Form)

After successfully blocking a punch, immediately seize the wrist of your opponent's attacking hand by trapping it against your chest, and apply pressure across the forearm (Fig. 16). While maintaining this wrist lock, lift your front leg and strike your opponent in the face with a right front kick (Fig. 17).

Fig. 18

Fig. 19

Fig. 20

Applying the Lotus Stance, Ground Grabbing Technique (Figs. 29–31 in the Form)

Once you have entered into close range, assume the lotus stance while maintaining a check on your opponent's lead hand (Fig. 18). Immediately upon dropping to the ground, grab the back of your opponent's lead leg with your right hand and the front of his leg with your left hand (Fig. 19). Take your opponent down by simultaneously pulling with your right hand and pushing with your left hand (Fig. 20)

Fig. 21

Fig. 22

Fig. 23

Fig. 24

Applying the Hammer Strike, Inverted Punch, Downward Chop (Figs. 32, 33, 37, 38, 42 in the Form)

As your opponent attacks with a right center punch, simultaneously block it with a left open-hand downward block while striking him in the face with a right hammer strike (Fig. 21). You attempt to follow this up by striking your opponent with an elbow strike to the face, which is blocked (Fig. 22). Immediately upon detecting that your strike has been intercepted, rotate your attacking arm counterclockwise and strike your opponent in the sternum with a right-hand inverted punch (Fig. 23). Your opponent then attempts to strike you with a right center punch, which you simultaneously block and counter with a right downward chop to his face (Fig. 24).

PART FOUR

Supplemental Training

10

The Weapons of Ngo Cho Kun

INTRODUCTION

It is often said that one anyone who wishes to practice kung-fu must first possess good character and perseverance. It is only through perseverance that one can become soft and gentle. It is only through gentleness that one can gain the self-control necessary to further achieve one's goal of greatness. Practitioners of ngo cho kun observe the creed:

- Do not be furious over your personal enemy, but fight for the people's common enemy
- Do not aim for personal vengeance, but root for the vengeance of the country
- Be righteous, and not afraid of hardships
- Do not draw your sword or attack at the slightest insult
- One must first learn to love oneself, before one can love one's country and its people

Through this attitude, one may achieve greatness not only for oneself, but one's country and its people. However, since it is not always possible to live life in harmony, skills in hand-to-hand combat must be developed. Part of those skills involve the use of various types of weapons. In theory, for one to effectively be able to defend against an armed opponent one must have an understanding of the make-up and use of various weapons. In ngo cho kun weapons are classified into two groups, wooden and metal.

WOODEN WEAPONS

Wooden weapons are generally referred to as staffs or clubs, with varying lengths of five, seven, nine, and twelve feet. When practicing club techniques it is important to stand in the *chien be* stance with the weapon

Monkey Pole

held central to the body *(chi ngo)*. To enable the weapon to strike the center of its intended target, the wielder's body must turn sideways. In ngo cho kun this is known as the single line body position *(it liao sin)*. It is also extremely important that one be precise in stepping, or fall prey to the possibility of striking oneself with one's weapon. When one maintains the proper form *(sze)*, strength and power will manifest themselves.

Club techniques are divided into soft and hard methods. Hard method club techniques include the upper and lower club methods, the single head club, the double head club, and the techniques of Emperor Sung Tai Cho and Tamo.

The upper club method of Master Lo Pan is delivered by striking straight down your opponent's center-line. To do this, one must swiftly evade an opponent's attack and then counter like a fierce tiger descending from the mountain, your strike descending like the downward pour of a waterfall. The power of this strike is awesome, and those unable to avoid it will be severely injured.

Techniques of the soft method include the lohan club, white crane club, and monkey pole. In the soft method, you accommodate your opponent's fighting posture or the path his chosen technique travels. If attacking down your opponent's center line proves difficult, the soft method

Peddler's Staff

7-Foot Staff

advises that you evade by turning from side to side. If your opponent attacks with the hard method, you must find an opening and swiftly enter into his space, thereby using the soft method to subdue the hard technique. Thus the old master's maxim: "Thwarting a thousand pounds with two catties."

METAL WEAPONS

Sijo Chua Giok Beng was proficient in the use of eighteen long and short metal weapons. The long weapons used in ngo cho kun include the knife *(kwan-to)*, horse cutting knife *(chan be to)*, plum flower lance *(muy hua chiu)*, sky halberd *(hong tian kiek)*, long spear hook *(kao liam chiu)*, mountain trident *(kai san pe)*, long and short club *(kun)*. As for the shortest weapons, there is the single broadsword *(tan-to)*, single sword *(tan kiam)*, double short sword *(sang kiam)*, double short whip *(sang te pi)*, double steel rod *(sang kan)*, double clutches *(tonfa)*, peddler's staff *(pinta)*, umbrella, sword and shield *(to pai wat)*.

Sai

Sai

The double short flog *(suang tuan pian)* was invented by the founder of ngo cho kun, Chua Giok Beng, and for nearly 100 years it has been handed down from generation to generation. It is considered a special type of weapon, and is rarely seen in kung-fu circles. The double short flog was a popular weapon in Fukien province in times past, as it was convenient to carry on either side of the waist. This alone made it a convenient and thus popular weapon for self-defense. There are four forms used to train in the double short flog. Each of the forms can be practice either alone or in practical application with a partner wielding a staff *(kun)* or horse cutting knife *(chan be to)*.

When fighting with weapons one must always be sure not to leave unattended the five gates of defense: high, middle, low, left, and right. The rule to follow in practicing with weapons is to practice diligently and regularly to hone your skills. The practice of kung-fu weapons serves not only as good physical exercise, but helps develop skills for practical armed defense should the need arise.

Horse Cutting Knife

Sword

Plum Spear

11

Iron Weight Strength Exercises

INTRODUCTION

The *chio so,* an iron weight shaped like an ancient Chinese lock, is a tool used in ngo cho kun for increasing arm strength and endurance. In ancient China, the *chio so* is generally made of stone. In the Philippines, because of the unavailability of hard stone, metal is used instead to make the *chio so.* There are many ways of training with the *chio so,* including solo and partner exercises.

For the novice, it is advisable to first practice lifting the *chio so* to chest level, bending the arm to gain momentum, and pushing the weight upward over the head. Then, return the *chio so* to chest level, bend the arm again, and lower the *chio so* to its starting position. Repeat the ascending and descending motions to strengthen the arm, thus increasing the power of your strikes and blocks. Another variation is to lift the *chio so* in front of you until it is level with your shoulders. After lowering the weight, lift it again from your sides until it is level with your shoulders. Practice doing these exercises, alternating between your front and your side. Once you are able to perform several repetitions of these initial exercises with ease you are ready to move on to the following three exercises.

IRON WEIGHT EXERCISES

The lock-shaped iron weight training *(chio so kung)* is used for conditioning the arms to develop strength and endurance. The *chio so* used in the following photographs weighs thirty kilograms, however you may want to begin your training with a twenty kilograms weight instead. These exercises are progressive and should be practiced in the order presented for safety and best results.

Twist and Catch Method

The twist and catch exercise requires concentration, timing, and focus.

It is not a simple exercise of mere upward and downward motions, but requires physical exertion since the twisting and throwing of the *chio so* should be done in a quick, single motion to prevent it from falling to the ground. You should be able to catch the *chio so* immediately upon throwing it 360-degrees clockwise.

To perform this exercise, stand in a horse stance, hold the *chio so* by the handle, and lift it upward to shoulder level (Fig. 1). Release the *chio so* by twisting and throwing it counterclockwise 360-degrees (Fig. 2), catching it immediately upon completion of the rotation (Fig. 3). After catching the weight, allow it to swing down before lifting it up to shoulder level again and repeating the sequence.

Usually, a single turn of the *chio so* is enough. Those who have reached the higher stages of *chio so* training will find that with only one single throw or twist, the *chio so* may turn two or more times. Nonetheless, the beginner should feel satisfied practicing with a single twist, as this itself is an accomplishment. The multiple twists may come later when one has reached the proficiency of a master.

A derivation of the front twist and catch method described above is the side twist and catch method. Once you can easily perform the front throws, proceed to the side throws which are more difficult. In addition, the side throw method is done to prepare you for the upward lift method.

The upward lift *chio so* method is performed by facing the front, holding the *chio so* by its handle, and throwing it upward. As the *chio so* descends, catch it with the back of your fist, like a landing port. Then proceed to throw it upward again from this balance position. As it falls, receive it again on the back of your fist. After spending some time perfecting this method you will be able to use other parts of your body, such as the arms and elbows, to receive, balance, and throw the *chio so*. After perfecting this series of exercises you may proceed to the next exercise, the back flowery throw and catch method.

Fig. 1   Fig. 2   Fig. 3

Fig. 4

Fig. 5

Fig. 6

Back Flowery Throw and Catch Method

To perform this exercise, stand in a horse stance, grab the *chio so* by the handle, and swing it behind you (Fig. 4). As your arm descends and then ascends in front of you, throw the *chio so* up above your shoulder (Fig. 5). As the weight descends in front of you, catch it by the handle as it reaches shoulder level (Fig. 6). Repeat the same procedure, this time using the left hand. When practicing this exercise the eyes, hands, and body should be coordinated as a miscalculation in your movements may cause injury to your head, waist, or ribs. To prevent this, lean or twist your body a little to the left as you are performing the exercise with the right hand, and vice versa. This is done as a precaution to establish a safe distance between your body and the weight, to avoid accidentally hitting yourself with the *chio so*.

Two Person Throwing Method

To perform the two person throwing exercise, stand facing your partner in a level horse stance and lift the *chio so* to shoulder level (Fig. 7). Next, twist and throw the weight to your partner so that it rotates 360-degrees in the air (Fig. 8). Your partner will catch the *chio so* (Fig. 9) and allow his arm to swing down with its momentum (Fig. 10). Upon catching the *chio so* your partner will lift it to shoulder level and twist and throw it back to you so that it rotates 360-degrees in the air (Fig. 11). Repeat the sequence as many times as you like.

It is advisable to practice the above exercises with both hands and to incrementally increase the weight of the *chio so* for maximum strength development and conditioning effects. If practiced diligently, the methods of the *chio so* take approximately two years to perfect.

Fig. 7

Fig. 8

Fig. 9

Fig. 10

Fig. 11

12

Partner Conditioning Exercises

Partner conditioning exercises play three important roles in the development of the ngo cho kun practitioner. First, they are intended to strengthen and toughen the inner and outer forearms, thus developing so-called "iron forearms." Second, they are used to instruct how to maintain the proper distance between you and your opponent when engaged in hand-to-hand combat. Third, they teach the practitioner to be unafraid of not only pain, but of being in close proximity to an opponent. The following are two of the basic empty-hand partner conditioning exercises practiced in ngo cho kun.

ARM HITTING EXERCISE

The instructions which follow should be followed identically by both partners. Prior to engaging in the arm hitting exercise, perform the *qi kun* (opening fist set). Begin the arm hitting exercise by facing your partner in a horse stance (the final movement of the opening fist set). Step forward with your right leg and strike your right forearm against your partner's (Fig. 1). Step back with your right leg then forward with your left leg and strike your left forearm against your partner's (Fig. 2). Step back with your left leg then forward with your right leg and swing your right arm across your body (fist pointing down), striking your right forearm against your partner's right forearm (Fig. 3). Step back with your right leg then forward with your left leg and swing your left arm across your body (fist pointing down), striking your left forearm against your partner's left forearm (Fig. 4). Next, step sideways with your left leg into a right *chien be* stance while swinging your right arm down, striking your right forearm against your partner's right forearm (Fig. 5). While maintaining your stance, swing your right arm upward assuming a right open-hand outside block, striking your forearm against your partner's forearm (Fig. 6). Follow this by immediately grabbing your partner's forearm

(Fig. 7). Next, pivot counterclockwise 180-degrees while blocking down, striking your left forearm against your partner's left forearm with a right-hand downward block (Fig. 8). While maintaining your stance, swing your left arm upward assuming a left open-hand outside block, striking your forearm against your partner's forearm (Fig. 9). Next, step backward with your left leg then forward with your right leg into a right *chien be* stance, and chop your right arm down and forward, striking the back of your opponent's forearm (Fig. 10). To complete the exercise, step back and assume a right hanging-leg stance, and close by assuming the *chiao yong* hands closing position (Fig. 11).

Fig. 1

Fig. 2

Fig. 3

Fig. 4

Fig. 5

Fig. 6

Fig. 7

Fig. 8

Fig. 9

Fig. 10

Fig. 11

GRAB AND PUNCH EXERCISE

The grab and punch exercise *(kim chieng wat)* of ngo cho kun is used as a means to develop block and counter-attack reflexes. In this exercise the *kim* (grab), *hian* (outside block), and *kai* (downward block) are performed in a continuous motion, immediately followed by stepping forward to punch (i.e., counter attack).

To begin this exercise, both partners should perform the *qi kun* (opening fist) set *(see* chap. 7, Figs. 1–8). Stand in preparation facing your partner in the final opening posture (Fig. 12). As your partner steps forward with his right leg and punches with his right hand, step back with your right leg and simultaneously block with your left arm and grab your opponent's forearm (Fig. 13). Quickly insert your right arm under your opponent's extended arm and perform an outside block while retracting your left hand (Figs. 14, 15). Next, parry your opponent's extended arm downward with your left arm, thus opening his defense (Fig. 16). Follow this up by stepping forward with your right leg and countering with a right punch to your opponent's chest (Fig. 17). The sequence now reverses, finding the attacker now defending and the defender now attacking (see Figs. 18–23).

Fig. 12

Fig. 13

Fig. 14

Fig. 15

Fig. 16

Fig. 17

Fig. 18

Fig. 19

Fig. 20

Fig. 21

Fig. 22

Fig. 23

Afterword

Although no single text alone is sufficient for one's development in a martial art, it is hoped that this book has given you an overview of the background, development, and foundation of the ngo cho kun system of kung-fu. I have attempted to offer this introductory book as a guide to show ngo cho kun to be a complete system of self-defense and a strong fighting art. Although this volume covers the foundation of the ngo cho kun system, it is in no way meant to be a substitute for a qualified instructor, whose instruction and guidance is essential for proper development in this Chinese martial art. Since ngo cho kun is also one of the primary Chinese martial arts which helped to form Okinawan karatedo, this book serves as an historical root showing the travel of martial arts from China to Okinawa. To perfect the techniques within, it is best to practice them in the order shown. For those interested in more information on the art of ngo cho kun, you may contact me care of the publisher. Best wishes on your new journey. May the beauty of this art influence your life as it has mine.

APPENDIX 1

The 44 Forms Ngo Cho Kun

sam chien (three wars tension)

tian te lin chian (heaven, earth, and man tension)

pieng ma chien (even stance tension)

cho chien wat (left tension)

ho chien wat (crane's tension)

tit kieng chien (straight bow tension)

lieng tao chien (dragon's head tension)

hong be chien (phoenix tail tension)

ngo ho chien (five tiger tension)

sui hwa chien (elegant tension)

li sip kun (twenty punches)

sang sou kun (double roundhouse punch)

se mun pa kak (hitting the four corners)

song sui kun (double banner fist)

sam chien sip li (three wars cross pattern)

se mun kwa (four direction sweep)

chian li ta (chopping attack)

tui chong (pursuing fist)

se mun cho tue (attacking the lower four directions)

se mun tiao cha (deflecting/intercepting the four directions)

cho be se mun kun (walking the four direction fist)

sip li kun (cross punch)

lak hap kun (six harmonious fists)

in tin tat (entwining kick)

liong gi (two segments)

sam chay (three segments)

se hong (fourth segments)

sa kak yiao (three corners rocking punch)

sam to tin to (three times hitting the head)

ngo to tim tao (five times hitting the head)

tiong kwan wat (controlling the center method)

sang plan wat (double whip strike)

wey ma yiao (turning stance rocking punch)

lian kwan pakua (linking the eight trigrams)

sang lieng po in (double dragon fist)

sai tze wan sin (lion body turning fist)

hi li po (child-holding-the-tablet fist)

hui ho sang liao (claws of the flying crane)

ko twi pi (drummer's flog)

pe guan chu tong (white ape exits from the cave)

chieng hong wat (cool breeze method)

sachap lak tian kong wat (36 steps of the monkey)

chi chap li tije swat wat (72 steps comet fist)

lien shia wat (the way of lien shia)

APPENDIX 2

Lineage of Ngo Cho Kun

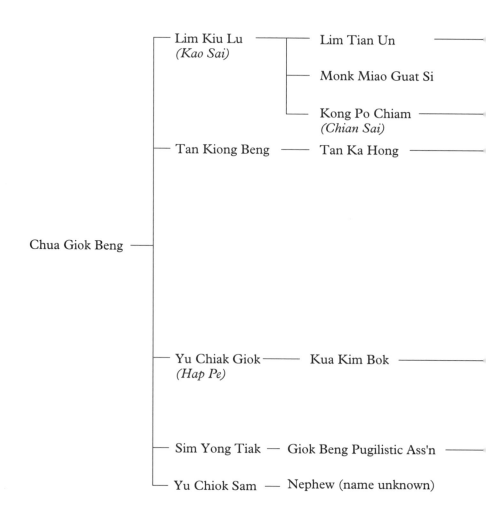

Chua Giok Beng

- Lim Kiu Lu
  (Kao Sai)
  - Lim Tian Un
  - Monk Miao Guat Si
  - Kong Po Chiam
    (Chian Sai)
- Tan Kiong Beng — Tan Ka Hong
- Yu Chiak Giok — Kua Kim Bok
  (Hap Pe)
- Sim Yong Tiak — Giok Beng Pugilistic Ass'n
- Yu Chiok Sam — Nephew (name unknown)

Chiu Tzu Kiong
(Kun Tao-ok)
— Chiu Beng Yan

— Chua Yi Sin

Lo Yan Chiu
(Ho Bu Chu)
— Phil-Kong Han
(Lo Keng Huy)
— Lo Si Beng
(Henry Lo)

Tan Kieng Tong
(Willian Tan)

— Beng Kian Athletic Ass'n

Tan Siao Tong
(Benito Tan)

Alfonso Ang
(Hua Kun)
— Tsing Hua Ngo Cho
Kung-fu Club

Alexander Lim Co — Mark Wiley

Willy Keh

Alfredo Ngo

Christopher Ricketts

Son (name unknown)

Ang Tun Kieng

Ku Ka Chiong — Hao Chun Tieng
(Pablo Hao)

— Beng Sing Pugilistic Ass'n

Glossary of Terms

bi lin sue cheng 美女梳妝 the lady-fixing-her-hair technique

bu siu chai 武秀才 a county-certified military officer. One can qualify for the post by passing a test of shooting an arrow into a target while astride a running horse

chang chuan 長拳 the long fist fighting style of Tai Cho kung-fu

che chat 坐節 the bending-the-joint movement

chi kung 氣功 exercises to develop internal energy

chi-ngo tiong ki 子午中肢 the center-arm, on-guard position, the characteristic fighting stance of ngo cho kun

chiao yong chiu 招揚手 the closing fist posture of the kun-to forms

chiat 切 slice chop

chien be 戰馬 the characteristic fighting stance of ngo cho kun

chien 戰 literally, battle, more accurately tension or trembling. It is called chien, war, because you are fighting within your own body to increase power.

chieng hong wat 清風法 cool breeze method

chieng lieng tiam 青龍點 green-dragon-spot technique

chio so 石鎖 lock-shaped iron weight

chiok tat 足踢 front kick

chiu kai 手開 downward block

cho chiu chiat 左手切 slice chop

cho chiu kim 左手擒 grabbing block

cho chiu muy hwe chiu 左手梅花槍 plum flower left-hand spear

cho kay 左開 elbow strike

chua kun 蛇拳 the snake fist style of kung-fu

Chuan Chiu 泉州 a city in Fukien province, China, where the ngo cho kun system of kung-fu originated

chuka 朱家 the southern Shaolin styles of kung-fu

chun chiu 駿手 the vibrating-the-hand movement

fu jow pai 虎瓜派 the tiger style of kung-fu

hi li po pai 孩兒抱牌 child-holding-the-tablet palm strike

ho liao 虎瓜 tiger claw strike

hong ko pua 風鼓劈 downward chop

hong tian kiek 方天戟 sky halberd weapon

Hung-gar 洪家 the tiger-crane style of kung-fu

in tin so 茵藤俊 the entwining grab technique

in tin tat 茵藤踢 the entwining kick fist form

kai san pe 開山鈀 mountain trident weapon
kak be 角馬 corner stance
kao kun 猴拳 monkey boxing
kao liam chiu 鉤鐮槍 long spear hook
Kwi Kieng thua 開弓彈
kia ka po 寄足步 hanging leg step (stance; toe stance)
kiao 撟 uppercut
kieng tzi be 弓箭馬 the bow-and-arrow stance
kim chian tuat kock 金蟬脫殼 the golden-cicada-shedding-its-skin technique
kim chieng wat 擒撞法
kim 擒 grab
kin kung 輕功 light body training/technique
kong 憤 hammer strike
kui kieng thua 開弓彈 open bow-snapping chop
kun-to 拳套 the fist forms of ngo cho kun
kut be chiu wat 屈馬手法
kut be kay 屈馬開 kneeling open-hand block
kut be po 屈馬步 crouched kneeling step
kut be sang li 屈馬雙擒 kneeling double splitting block
kut be so 屈馬俊 kneeling grab
kut be 屈馬 half-kneeling position
Kwan Peng po in 關平抱印 the General Kwan Peng-holding-the-seal movement
kwi chian 關剪 scissors block

lek si tun 力士擋 ground grabbing technique
lian chiong kung 練掌功 palm slapping exercise
lian kuan sao kua chiu 建環掃掛手 continuous cutting hand sweep
Lin Gi Tong 仁義堂 literally, "Hall of Justice." The name of Chua Giok Beng's kung-fu club

Lin Tek Tong 仁德堂 literally, "Hall of Humanity." The name given by Chua Giok Beng for Tan Kiong Beng's kung-fu club. It is customary in kung-fu that the master name the club for his disciple as a gesture of approval.
lohan 羅漢 the internal fighting techniques of the Shaolin arhat monks

mui hwe chiu 梅花槍 plum flower lance

nei-ching 內勁 intrinsic energy
ngo cho kun 五祖拳 the Amoy language pronunciation of the fists of the five ancestors system of kung-fu.
ngo ki lat 五肢力 the integration of five parts power, which includes the head, hands, and feet.

pa kua 八卦 the eight-trigram style of internal kung-fu
pa chat 打節 elbow striking technique
pan-ngi-nang 半硬軟 Fukienese term for half-hard and half-soft (kung-fu)
pat-wat 八法 Chua Giok Beng's eight-method deadly technique
peho 白鶴 the fighting style of Fukien white crane kung-fu
peng kai 並開 scooping block
peng tioh 並挑 outside block
peng wan tui 並右手削 inverted punch
peng yu chiu sia 鐵沙掌 side chop
pian 鞭 backfist, or whip strike
pu 步 the float concept
puan chian wat 盤剪法 the scissors kick take down technique, also known as the lion turning the body technique

qi kun 起拳 the opening fist set of ngo cho kun empty-hand forms

sai-ah wan sin 獅仔翻身 the lion turning the body technique, also known as the scissors kick take down *sam chien* 三戰 three wars form

sang cha 雙插 double finger thrust technique

sang chiu te ki 雙 double short-hand techniques used in ngo cho kun

sang chiu tung ki 雙 double long-hand techniques 間sed in ngo cho kun

sang kan 雙釭 double steel rod

sang kia kun 雙堅拳 double straight punch

sang kiam 雙劍 double swords

sang kiao chiu 雙橋手 double upper-cut

sang kwa 雙掛 double hook blocking technique

sang kwa chiu 雙掛手 double palm strike

sang kwan kun 雙貫拳 double pen-etrating uppercut

sang kwi chian 雙關剪 double clos-ing scissors block

sang lieng chiu tsu 雙龍搶珠 the double-dragon-fighting-for-the-pearl technique

sang lieng tiam taw 雙龍點頭 the double green-dragon-spot technique

sang pueh 雙批 double chop

sang te pi 雙短鞭 double short whip

sang tit teh 雙直退 double backward step

sao kua chiu 捎掛手 cutting hand sweep

shen 神 soul

si pieng be 四平馬 level horse stance

siam be po 閃馬步 evading step

sifu 師父 the master of a Chinese mar-tial art

sigung 師公 the grandmaster of a Chi-nese martial art

sihing 師兄 a practitioner's older brother (classmate) in kung-fu

sijo 師祖 the founder of a Chinese mar-tial art

siu kun 收拳 the closing fist set of ngo cho kun empty-hand forms

siu po pai 收抱牌 the closing fist pos-ture of the chien forms

suang tuan pian 雙短鞭 name of the weapon known in karate as the sai

ta yu chiak 踏右足 the forward step

ta-po 踏步 the step-on stance

Tai Cho 太祖 the kung-fu technqiues of Emperor Sang Tai Cho

tai peng 大鵬 the roc-spreading-its-wings technique

tan chiu te ki 單 single short hand techniques found in ngo cho kun

tan chiu tung ki 單 single long hand techniques found in ngo cho kun

tan to 單刀 broadsword or saber

tang lang 螳螂 the Praying mantis style of kung-fu

tap be po 楊馬步 overlapping step

tap che lian hiong yu 楊坐蓮向右 lo-tus posture

te bok sut 地犬術 the dog style of kung-fu

ti sha chiong 鐵 iron palm exercises/technique

ti tui tim kong 鐵槌沈江 the metal-hammer-sinking-in-the-river move-ment

tiap chin po 疊進步 double forward step

tim 沈 the sink concept

tiong hua yu sut tai tsuan 中華柔術大全

tiong kuk bu sut 中國武術 an anti-quated term for Chinese martial arts

tit chin sang kue chian 直進雙關剪 double scissors block

tit chieng kun 直撞拳 straight punch

tit chin po 直進步 direct forward step

tit teh po 直退步 backward step

tit-teh 直退 direct backward step

to pai wat 刀牌法 sword and shield

tok 啄 finger strike

tsay tui 踩腿 cutting kick

tu 吐 the spit out concept

tueh 釵 side straight chop

tui 腿 straight side thrust

tun 吞手 the swallow concept

tun chiu 吞 the swallowing -he-hand movement

wu chu chuan 五租拳 the Mandarin

pronunciation of the fists of the five ancestors system of kung-fu

ying jow pai 鷹瓜派 the eagle claw style of kung-fu

yu chiu kong 右手憤 hammer strike

yu chiu tok 右手啄 finger strike

yu chiu tue 右手釵 straight side thrust

Famous Ngo Cho Kun Masters

Tan Ka Hong 陳家鴻
Tan Kiong Beng 陳京銘
Chua Giok Beng 蔡玉鳴
Chang Tzi Chiang 張之江

Chang Hun Chiong 張雲章
Lim Tian Suy 林天水
Miao Gwat Si 妙月師